T0286958

Cambridge Elements ≡

Elements in the Politics of Development
edited by
Rachel Beatty Riedl
Einaudi Center for International Studies and Cornell University
Ben Ross Schneider
Massachusetts Institute of Technology

Mario Einaudi
CENTER FOR
INTERNATIONAL STUDIES

 MIT CENTER FOR INTERNATIONAL STUDIES

CLAIM-MAKING IN COMPARATIVE PERSPECTIVE

Everyday Citizenship Practice and Its Consequences

Janice K. Gallagher
Rutgers University
Gabrielle Kruks-Wisner
University of Virginia
Whitney K. Taylor
San Francisco State University

Shaftesbury Road, Cambridge CB2 8EA, United Kingdom

One Liberty Plaza, 20th Floor, New York, NY 10006, USA

477 Williamstown Road, Port Melbourne, VIC 3207, Australia

314–321, 3rd Floor, Plot 3, Splendor Forum, Jasola District Centre, New Delhi – 110025, India

103 Penang Road, #05–06/07, Visioncrest Commercial, Singapore 238467

Cambridge University Press is part of Cambridge University Press & Assessment, a department of the University of Cambridge.

We share the University's mission to contribute to society through the pursuit of education, learning and research at the highest international levels of excellence.

www.cambridge.org
Information on this title: www.cambridge.org/9781009517812

DOI: 10.1017/9781009028820

First published 2024

A catalogue record for this publication is available from the British Library.

ISBN 978-1-009-51781-2 Hardback
ISBN 978-1-009-01392-5 Paperback
ISSN 2515-1584 (online)
ISSN 2515-1576 (print)

Claim-Making in Comparative Perspective

Everyday Citizenship Practice and Its Consequences

Elements in the Politics of Development

DOI: 10.1017/9781009028820
First published online: February 2024

Janice K. Gallagher
Rutgers University

Gabrielle Kruks-Wisner
University of Virginia

Whitney K. Taylor
San Francisco State University

Author for correspondence: Gabrielle Kruks-Wisner, gkk5x@virginia.edu

Abstract: Claim-making – the everyday strategies through which citizens pursue rights fulfillment – is often overlooked in studies of political behavior, which tend to focus on highly visible, pivotal moments: elections, mass protests, high court decisions, legislative decisions. But what of the politics of the everyday? This Element takes up this question, drawing together research from Colombia, South Africa, India, and Mexico. The authors argue that claim-making is a distinct form of citizenship practice characterized by its everyday nature, which is neither fully programmatic nor clientelistic; and which is prevalent in settings marked by gaps between the state's de jure commitments to rights and their de facto realization. Under these conditions, claim making is both meaningful (there are rights to be secured) and necessary (fulfillment is far from guaranteed). Claim-making of this kind is of critical consequence, both materially and politically, with the potential to shape how citizens engage (or disengage) the state.

This Element also has a video abstract: www.Cambridge.org/Kurks

Keywords: claim-making, rights, state–society relations, citizenship practice, feedback effects

ISBNs: 9781009517812 (HB), 9781009013925 (PB), 9781009028820 (OC)
ISSNs: 2515-1584 (online), 2515-1576 (print)

Contents

Introduction

Cali, Colombia. In a low-income neighborhood, a woman struggling to access care for her asthma turned to the courts to file a claim to Colombia's constitutionally recognized right to health. She did so through the *acción de tutela*, a procedure that enables direct appeals. "Everything happens through the tutela," she explained.[1] Across the country, in Bogotá, a man echoed this: "Before the tutela, there was nothing one could do. It was necessary to wait for a politician to be elected, and if he cared about that community, wait for him to intervene in some way. Not now. Now, an individual, a single person, can file a complaint with the tutela."[2]

Durban, South Africa. Residents of informal settlements across KwaZulu-Natal, facing eviction following the 2007 "Slums Act," turned to a variety of methods to contest their impending displacement, from local organizing, to protests, to legal claim-making. In the end, their legal claims were what stayed the evictions; the South African Constitutional Court ruled in favor of the residents, finding that the Slums Act was in violation of the constitutional right to access to adequate housing. As one resident stated, "Luckily, our courts were there with us."[3]

Rajasthan, India. In a remote village, a group of women had labored for months at a government construction site, only to learn that they were not being paid their full wage. Angry, they went to the\ *Gram Sevak* – a local administrator overseeing the public works program – to demand access to payment records. In another village close by, women discussing the lack of reliable drinking water decided to visit their *panchayat* (local council) meetings to complain. One woman recalled: "At first you might feel shy . . . . But you cannot sit *chup-chup* (quiet) . . . the meetings are where we can raise our voices to the concerned officials."[4]

Monterrey, Mexico. A diverse group of women gathered on the steps of the State Attorney General's office. Most were searching for their children who had been disappeared during Mexico's surge in violent crime. They would spend the day in *mesas de trabajo* (participatory working groups) with investigators, police, and officials from state and federal bureaucracies. While expectations that these meetings would lead to finding their loved ones or prosecuting those responsible remained low, one participant expressed: "What option do we have? Before, they would treat us so badly, and never do anything. Now, at least, we are talking."[5]

***

---

[1] Taylor interview, Cali, April 9, 2017.   [2] Taylor interview, Bogotá, March 15, 2016.
[3] Taylor interview, Durban, November 29, 2017.
[4] Kruks Wisner interview, Udaipur, December 16, 2010.
[5] Gallagher interview, Monterrey, February 7, 2012.

What do these stories, drawn from different corners of the world, have in common? At first glance, they are strikingly different, moving from rural villages to large metropoles, and from individual to collective action on issues ranging from basic services to fundamental human rights. All, though, represent a critical – but surprisingly overlooked – arena of politics: everyday claim-making by citizens. In each of these cases, citizens are actively pursuing resources, services, and protection – social and physical – from the state. They are, moreover, seeking redress where public commitments have been broken; legally established rights to healthcare, to housing, to water, and to physical integrity and due legal process have not been realized. In all cases, ordinary citizens, including some of the poorest and most marginalized, have turned to administrative or judicial arenas staffed by bureaucrats, judges, investigators, and other state functionaries. They have met with mixed, and in some cases limited, success; not all demands have been heard and not all problems have been resolved. But in each case, citizens have taken steps to narrow the gap between the promises and actions of the state.

Everyday citizenship practice of this kind – that is, the strategies through which citizens make claims on the state in their day-to-day lives – are often overlooked in studies of political behavior, which tend to focus on highly visible, pivotal moments: elections, mass protests, high court decisions, the passing of significant legislation. But what of the politics of the everyday? This Element takes up this question, drawing together accounts from Latin America, South Asia, and sub-Saharan Africa. Together, as authors, we are motivated by our collective observation that much of the dominant literature on political participation does not fully capture the everyday efforts of citizens, who doggedly seek to engage the state beyond the ballot and the barricade. Most scholarship on distributive politics tends to focus either on efforts to affect programmatic policy change through voting (Garay 2016; Iversen 2005) or social movement mobilization (McAdam et al. 2001; Tarrow 1998), or on clientelistic exchange between citizens and politicians (Grossman and Slough 2022; Stokes et al. 2013). Everyday claim-making, however, does not fit neatly into any of these modes.

Before coming together to write this Element, each of us in our individual bodies of work observed forms of citizen–state engagement unfolding beyond elections, below movements, and in manners that were neither programmatic nor strictly clientelistic. Taylor, for example, found that neither electoral nor social movement studies could explain how the rights to health or to housing have become institutionalized in Colombia and South Africa; nor could they explain the legal mobilization of citizens through courts to claim those rights. In rural India, Kruks-Wisner similarly found that explanations centered solely on political parties fell short in accounting for the high but varied levels of claim-making she observed among citizens seeking welfare goods and services; nor were these patterns the direct result of sustained social movement activity. Gallagher also observed that the interactions between officials and families affected by drug war violence in Mexico did not fall easily into the category of social movement mobilization: while such mobilization certainly occurred, it didn't define these dynamics. She knew, moreover, that political parties had little to do with the intensive and significant investigatory work being done by victims' collectives along with state investigators and prosecutors.

Each of us became convinced that we were observing something central to citizenship practice, as well as to distributive politics. Direct, day-to-day encounters with actors in the bureaucracy and judiciary were having a profound effect in shaping citizens' expectations of and engagements with the state. Those same encounters were critical in shaping citizens' access to resources, as well as broader patterns of inequality. As we began to share our research, we noted that the distributive consequences of claim-making were mixed. Claim-making was, for some, a means of securing essential goods, services, and protections. It was, in these cases, a way forward (at times halting or inching) toward closing the gap between the promises and actions of the state. Claimants, we observed, came from an array of social positions not strictly defined by class, caste, or other markers of socioeconomic status. The stakes, however, appeared highest for the most disadvantaged: those who could least take access to public resources for granted, and to whom the state was often the least responsive. Claim-making, moreover, was not costless; it carried risks, and required investments of time, resources, and skill. Nor did it always work, leaving many claims unanswered. The resulting unevenness, both in terms of which citizens made claims and in how effectively they did so, could deepen inequalities between citizens with varying resources, capacity, and access to the state. Yet, claim-making could also mitigate inequality by providing inroads for those who lacked the political or social connections to make their voices heard through other channels.

In what follows, we seek to highlight, theorize, and probe these everyday engagements, drawing together our individual bodies of research in and with communities in Colombia, South Africa, India, and Mexico. We have two objectives in writing this Element. Our first is theory building: to reflect on the specificities of our cases, as well as their commonalities, to develop and explore the concept of claim-making. Our aims are to call attention to the prevalence and importance of quotidian acts of claim-making; to examine the conditions that give rise and shape to these politics; and to reflect on their material, distributive, and political consequences. Our second objective is agenda setting: to lay the groundwork for future engagement with and research on the concept of claim-making well beyond our study sites.

Questions and Arguments

We set out to investigate three sets of questions. First, what is claim-making and who are citizen claimants? Second, what enables and provokes claim-making, and why does this mode of participation appear to be particularly prevalent across low-to-middle income democracies? Third, why and how does claim-making matter, both materially (for distributive politics) and politically (for citizen–state relations)? In exploring these questions, we make three arguments.

First, we define claim-making broadly as citizens' quotidian engagement of the state in pursuit of rights and entitlements. Claim-making, we argue, is a form of citizenship practice distinct from voting, from clientelism, and from large-scale social movement mobilization; it is characterized by its everyday as well as often direct nature, which is neither fully programmatic nor fully clientelistic. Claim-making occurs when citizens engage in bureaucratic and judicial arenas to seek services and fulfillment of rights. The goods, services, and protections to which citizens lay claims are rarely distributed in a rule-bound fashion that directly reflects written law and policy. Neither, though, are they necessarily or simply the subjects of partisan exchange; political parties are not the sole or even central actors mediating citizens' access. Claim-making is an "in-between" act, falling between programmatic and clientelist modes of exchange, as well as between and beyond elections and mass mobilization. It is this "in-between" status, we suggest, that has led to claim-making's relative neglect as a subject of inquiry, as it has been seen as tangential or ancillary to more studied realms of participation. By delineating claim-making as its own, distinct form of citizenship practice, we seek to highlight both its prevalence and importance, as well as to consider its interplay with other modes of electoral and non-electoral participation.

Second, we argue that claim-making practices are likely to develop where the state's institutional terrain is both *broad* (the state is visible and central to citizens' lives) and *irregular* (the state is inconsistent in its distribution of resources and fulfillment of rights). These uneven conditions are marked by a pronounced gap between de jure commitments to social, economic, and civil rights and their de facto realization. Such gaps are present across a range of low-to-middle income democracies, spurred by simultaneous and seemingly contradictory waves of rights expansion and state retrenchment. Across our cases, we observe how constitutional and other legal reforms have broadened states' formal commitments to their citizens, leading to the creation of new and expanding institutions – courts, local hearings and deliberative bodies, social audits, grievance platforms – through which citizens can seek fulfillment and redress. At the same time, cuts in spending and the hollowing out of state capacity have limited the depth and regularity with which many of the same states can meet their formal commitments. This sets the stage for claim-making, as citizens are *pushed* by necessity to pursue rights claims, and are simultaneously *pulled* into institutional fora created for the purposes of claim-making.

Third, we argue that claim-making practices are of critical consequence, both *materially* (visible, albeit variably, in benefits secured and rights upheld) and *politically*, with the potential to shape what citizens expect and how they engage (or disengage) the state. We employ a feedback loop framework to explore the ways in which state responsiveness can lead to ongoing claim-making and how non-responsiveness might deter engagement. We argue that many feedback effects are neither positive nor negative but ambivalent, as partial state responsiveness, combined with the crucial nature of claimants' needs, propel ongoing engagement even when the rewards of such action are sporadic. As a whole, we argue that the consequences of claim-making are of critical importance to citizens' lives and that these engagements are central to the way an increasingly large number of citizens experience the state. Claim-making carries distributive consequences, influencing who has access to goods, services, and protections; over time, claim-making may also prompt qualitative changes in how state institutions respond to citizens' needs.

Cases and Contextualized Comparison

In building these arguments, we draw together original data and narratives from our respective fieldwork sites. We pull upon a rich combination of qualitative and quantitative methods, from in-depth interviews, original surveys, and analyses of legal claims in Colombia and South Africa; to interviews and original surveys of rural residents and village-level case studies in India; to embedded ethnography, an original survey and analyses of legal data, and life history interviews in Mexico. Each of us builds on accumulated years of experience in our research sites, allowing us collectively to draw on in-depth analyses across a wide range of settings that a single author could not. Our aim is to map both similar and divergent claim-making practices and, by extension, patterns of citizen–state relations across different regional and institutional contexts.

Within each country, we narrow our attention to particular sectors, focusing on different rights, services, or protections. Our respective bodies of work are therefore best understood as comprising "*country-issue*" cases. In three of our cases, claim-making unfolds around social rights: to health (in Colombia); to housing (in South Africa); to work and welfare (in India). In our study of Mexico, claim-making is centered around the civil and political rights involved in combating impunity in cases of disappearances.

In **Colombia**, Taylor studied citizens' pursuit of the right to healthcare using the *acción de tutela* procedure – a legal mechanism created by the 1991 Constitution that allows individuals to ask judges to investigate potential violations of fundamental constitutional rights. By the end of 2019, Colombian citizens had filed roughly 7.9 million claims using the tutela. Individuals, rather than collective actors, file the majority of these claims,[6] which can be made without the support of a lawyer or any legal assistance. Judges must respond to these claims within ten days. Since 2003, between 23 and 40 percent of all tutela claims each year have involved the right to health.[7] Initially, however, the right to health was not considered to be a "fundamental" right, thus rendering it outside the scope of the tutela. Over time, judges expanded the purview of the tutela, and by 2008 the right to health was recognized as a fundamental constitutional right. Filing a tutela claim is now understood to be part of the process of accessing healthcare. To document and explore these patterns of legal claim-making in Colombia, Taylor drew from interviews with 92 "legal elites" (judges, clerks, lawyers, and law professors), as well as 93 everyday citizens, a 310-person survey of tutela claimants, and an analysis of 1,260 randomly sampled tutela claims.[8]

In **South Africa**, Taylor examined litigation for the right to housing. South Africa is hailed as an exemplar of socioeconomic rights protections with its expansive constitutional protections and robust Constitutional Court. Between 1996, when the Court began, and 2019, social rights cases comprised about 9.5 percent of the Court's work; about half of all social rights cases involve the right to housing. Typically an individual or group backed by NGOs, legal clinics, or pro bono lawyers advances these housing rights claims. Broader movement actors may also become involved with particular legal cases, but do not systematically drive the turn to legal claim-making. The Court has focused on bolstering protections for those who face evictions, striking down provincial legislation and requiring that the state provide "alternative accommodation" for those evicted from public or private land. While many still live in precarious and inadequate housing, claim-making has fundamentally reshaped policy around housing and evictions in South Africa. Taylor gained insight into these

---

[6] In a random sample of tutela claims reviewed by the Constitutional Court between 1992 and 2016, 85 percent were filed by individual claimants (Taylor 2020a).
[7] Comprehensive, disaggregated data on tutela claims are not available before 2003.
[8] See Taylor (2023a 2018, 2020a) for detailed methodology.

dynamics by conducting interviews with 88 current and former Constitutional Court justices and clerks, other lawyers and judges, and members of civil society involved in claim-making, in addition to fielding a survey of 551 individuals from three provinces and analyzing social rights cases.[9]

In **India**, Kruks-Wisner explored the strategies of citizens seeking access to an array of economic and social rights. Since the mid-2000s, India has seen an "unprecedented expansion of rights-based welfare" (Adhikari and Heller 2022), visible in new social policies related to the rights to food, work, and education, as well as other forms of social protection. These policies have been accompanied by new spaces for citizen claim-making, including deliberative fora at the village level, public hearings and social audits of government programs, and new mechanisms for grievance redressal. Kruks-Wisner explored the ways in which citizens engage this shifting landscape through a study of rural villages across the state of Rajasthan. Drawing on more than 500 interviews and a survey of 2,210 individuals across 105 villages, she found that a large majority (more than three-quarters) reported engaging in efforts to secure welfare goods and services from public officials.[10] The bulk of this activity unfolded at the local level, often through the *Gram Panchayat* – an elected (nominally nonpartisan) governing body that is also a key arena in which citizens encounter administrators and frontline government workers. Elsewhere in India, Kruks-Wisner has explored citizens' engagement in grievance hearings,[11] as well as the claim-making at rural block development offices – a middle tier of bureaucratic administration that oversees a wide range of government programs and entitlements.[12]

In **Mexico**, Gallagher spent more than a decade studying how citizens respond to the evolving crisis of disappearances within Mexico's escalating drug war. Since 2006, more than 100,000 people have been disappeared[13] in Mexico. The state has proved largely unable or unwilling to investigate victims' whereabouts or prosecute those responsible. In response, a small but vocal group of family members of the disappeared have engaged in efforts to compel the state to combat impunity and to fulfill rights to truth and justice. Individual claimants regularly engage with officials located across Mexico's Kafkaesque justice system, making demands on local, state, and national officials within a host of bureaucracies, including human rights commissions, commissions

---

[9] See Taylor (2020a, b) for detailed methodology.
[10] See Kruks-Wisner (2018a) for detailed methodology.   [11] See Kruks-Wisner (2021).
[12] See Kruks-Wisner and Kumar (2023).
[13] A person is considered "*disappeared*" rather than missing when there is reason to believe that their absence is involuntary – that is, that they were abducted, physically harmed, and/ or are being imprisoned and held against their will. See Gallagher (2023) for further discussion.

dedicated to searching for the disappeared, and various prosecutors' offices. Groups of family members have formed more than 100 collectives, the majority of which have established *mesas de trabajo* (participatory investigations) with state investigators and police. In these *mesas*, agreements are made about who will take investigatory actions, and officials are held to account for prior promises. Gallagher documented the evolution of this claim-making by embedding with human rights organizations and victims' collectives; building an original database of disappearances; conducting a nationally representative citizen survey; and filing scores of information requests for judicial results. She has worked in 18 of Mexico's 32 states, conducted more than 250 interviews with civil society leaders, families affected by disapperances, and state officials.

At first glance, these cases may seem to share few points of similarity. A citizen who turns to the state to seek a clean source of drinking water might seem worlds apart from one who demands that the police search for a missing son or husband. We, however, see all of our cases as examples of citizen contestation over the allocation of public resources. We therefore understand them as cases of *distributive politics*, extending not only to the allocation of monies and materials but also to forms of social and physical protection. Across our cases, citizens strive to extract resources and catalyze action by state officials, whether to provide drinking water, pay for healthcare, forestall evictions, or investigate disappearances. The divergent nature of what citizens are seeking from the state, and the highly different institutional contexts in which they are sought (from courts, to police stations, to local government offices), serves, in our view, to focus attention on what they have in common. All, simply put, are stories of citizens turning to the state to meet basic needs and fulfill fundamental rights. In each case, the good, service, or protection being sought is urgent and critical to their well-being. And in each case, citizens turn directly to public agencies and appointed state personnel to make their claims.

Our country-issue cases were not selected with comparison in mind. They were the settings and topics of each of our independent research far before the idea for this Element emerged. Our aim, therefore, is not to engage in "controlled comparisons" along purposively matched dimensions. Instead, we employ ex post methods of "contextualized comparison" (Locke and Thelen 1995; Simmons and Smith 2017) to integrate our accounts from different regions. We look deeply into and across our cases in order to distill what is common about claim-making in these varied sectors and institutional settings.

While we consciously do not employ a "most different" case logic, we use the differences across our country-issue cases to consider how the varied nature of grievances, the structure of institutions, and the presence of intermediaries, like parties and movements, might give shape to varieties of claim-making, and to explore how claim-making takes on different meanings in different contexts. The Colombian context offers the opportunity to examine claim-making in a particularly open institutional environment, which enables individuals to make direct, unmediated legal claims. The South African institutional context necessitates a more involved role for social movements and NGO brokers, which allows us to explore both individual and collective claim-making that is mediated by social actors. The case of welfare rights in India allows us to investigate claim-making in a setting where courts are weaker, but where citizens directly engage a wide range of administrative and bureaucratic actors, as well as party brokers and other intermediaries. Finally, our inclusion of the case of disappearances in Mexico allows us to probe both individual and group claim-making dynamics around a set of civil and political rights – extending our analysis across different rights arenas. Contextualized comparison allows for this exploration, without erroneously assuming that "the same practice has the same meaning or valence across the various countries" (Locke and Thelen 1995, p. 340).

While we focus in this Element on contemporary claim-making practices across these four country-issue cases, we do not suggest that claim-making is a new: claim-making in some form has existed since governments began making promises to their citizens. We posit, though, that this under-studied form of participation is becoming increasingly central to citizens' repertoires of action, in particular in settings where citizens grapple with unmet legal promises and commitments. Our deep engagements in Colombia, South Africa, India, and Mexico allow us to probe the contours of claim-making across four populous, diverse, and unequal low-to-middle income democracies, while also exploring how practices vary across different institutional settings. We do not, however, see claim-making as limited to our particular study sites, or to the so-called "global south." Similar dynamics are visible in settings around the globe in countries and communities at varying levels of development.

Roadmap

This Element is organized into three sections. Section 1 draws on accounts from Colombia, South Africa, India, and Mexico to argue that claim-making constitutes a unique type of political engagement, distinct from other participatory acts like voting or movement mobilization. Section 2 examines the conditions that have given rise to these practices, arguing that claim-making is most likely under "uneven" conditions where the state's reach as provider of services and guarantor of rights is both *broad* (visible and central to citizens' lives) and *irregular* unequal in the realization of its obligations). Section 3 reflects on the consequences of everyday claim-making, demonstrating its impact in citizens' lives while also noting the ways in which claims are stymied or ignored. We argue that whether or not citizens make claims on the state, and whether or not those claims are heard, play a powerful role in shaping citizens' expectations and longer-term (dis)engagement with the state. We conclude by reflecting on the contours of a broader research agenda for the study of claim-making, which we see as critical to an understanding of political participation and distributive politics worldwide.

1 Claimants and Claim-Making

In this section, we seek to distill and theorize the concept of claim-making. We begin by delineating the subjects (or content) of the claims in question. We then describe claim-making practices across our cases, highlighting the ways in which citizens approach officials in bureaucratic and judicial institutions. We go on to situate claim-making alongside other forms of participation that also seek to influence the implementation of policy, enforcement of law, and alloca-tion of public resources. We do so by offering a reconceptualization of types of distributive politics that account for the spaces between programmatic (rule-bound) and non-programmatic (non-rule bound, often partisan) politics. Finally, we consider the interplay between direct citizen claim-making and other, mediated approaches that engage political parties and social brokers.

From Citizenship Rights to Claim-Making

A claimant is a person or group of persons who approaches the state to seek an entitlement, service, or protection that they feel is due to them but which is unrealized. The content of their claims therefore centers on citizenship rights, which we broadly understand, following T.H. Marshall (1950), along civil, political, and social dimensions. Our cases are all settings that are procedurally democratic, where citizens enjoy at least a minimum level of political rights.[14] Our focus in this Element is therefore on claim-making centered on civil and social rights that extend beyond, though are intertwined with, the rights to democratic participation and representation. Civil rights, as defined by Marshall (1950, p. 148), encompass the right to justice ("to defend and assert all one's rights on terms of equality with others and by due process of law"), and legal protections of fundamental human rights such as the right to life and bodily integrity. Social rights, following Marshall (1950, p. 149), are cultural ("the right to share to the full in the social heritage") and economic ("the right to a modicum of economic welfare and security . . . and to live the life of a civilized being accordance to the standards prevailing in the society").

Not all such commitments are articulated in explicitly rights-based language; they can also be communicated through social policy, state directives, and the design of public programs. In all such cases, though, there is a de jure commitment – a promise based on law or policy – to the provision of a good, service, or protection. Claim-making unfolds when those commitments are

---

[14] We recognize, however, the frequent gaps between procedural guarantees and the substantive exercise of democracy. We also recognize that claim-making occurs in authoritarian contexts – although such settings fall beyond the scope of this Element. See the Conclusion for further discussion.

unrealized; that is, when there is a gap between de jure commitments and their de facto fulfillment. Claim-making, in this sense, both reflects and responds to the state as the guarantor of rights. The state sets the stage for claim-making through its commitments to particular entitlements and protections. Our country-issue cases therefore highlight specific rights that are salient in particular institutional contexts. A constitutional guarantee of the right to health in Colombia, for example, expanded the legal rights of citizens and the corresponding terrain for claim-making, as did the right to housing in South Africa, a guarantee of employment in India, and expanding legal entitlements for the disappeared and their families in Mexico. In all of these instances, formal administrative and judicial spaces were created or adapted to facilitate the fulfillment of newly articulated or reaffirmed rights.

Citizens turn to these spaces to engage in claim-making, navigating the policies, procedures, and people (judges, clerks, grievance officers, investigators, and other state functionaries) that they see as standing between themselves and the fulfillment of their rights. This is not, however, exclusively or even predominantly the practice of the poorest and most marginalized (although, as we discuss in Section 3, the stakes of claim-making are often higher for those groups). Claim-making can be engaged by the rich and poor alike, and can both challenge and reinforce patterns of inequality. The question of *who* makes claims, and whether they do so from a place of relative privilege or marginalization, rests in large part on *what* is being claimed. This varies across our four country-issue cases. In Mexico, families from all walks of life have suffered drug war violence and the disappearances of their loved ones. Victims' families – including those from relatively elite backgrounds – must doggedly pursue officials to demand investigation and legal action. In Colombia, the constitutional right to health often does not translate into access to affordable medications, and citizens must go to court to force insurance companies to cover those drugs. These practices are undertaken by a relatively wide swath of the population, including those from both the lower and middle classes.[15] In South Africa, in contrast, the right to housing – which has largely been interpreted as a way to forestall evictions – is almost entirely articulated by the urban poor in informal settlements. In rural India, poorer claimants are the most likely to seek access to poverty-alleviation programs. A newly established right to work, for example, created opportunities for minimum

---

[15] Taylor's 2017 survey of individuals waiting to file tutela claims in Medellín found, for example, that about 67 percent identified as being from the lower classes and 31 percent from the lower-middle or middle classes (Taylor 2018). Other studies focused specifically on the right to health have concluded that claim-making lags for the unemployed and informally employed (Landau 2014; Uprimny Yepes and Durán 2014).

wage labor on government work sites that are most often sought out by the poor. Other rural claimants seek services of importance to those of all class backgrounds: drinking water, for example, which is the subject of almost continuous claim-making in rural villages by residents of varied socioeconomic standing.

In all of these examples, claim-making is possible because there is – on paper – a commitment to a right or entitlement. In each case, claim-making is necessary because that right is unrealized. Claim-making is therefore best understood as the citizen-led work of realizing the state's rights commitments.

In developing this conception of claim-making, we build on a rich scholarship on participation and accountability that extends beyond the electoral to what Collier and Handlin (2009, p. 8) refer to as the "interest arena."[16] This "considerably more informal locus of specific interest articulation and problem solving" encompasses wide-ranging demands from citizens for the fulfillment, reinterpretation, and adoption of rights. We situate claim-making within this broad category of interest articulation, focusing on quotidian attempts to narrow the gap between existing promises and the lived reality of administrative neglect. Our notion of everyday claim-making is, in this regard, close to what Houtzager and Acharya (2011, p. 10) call active citizenship: "any attempt to hold agents of the state – i.e., public bureaucracy – directly accountable for meeting legal obligations to provision mandated public goods and services."[17] We take de jure rights and entitlements – expressed in law and policy but unrealized in citizens' lives – as the start point for claim-making. Our notion of claim-making is therefore also proximate to O'Brien's notion of "rightful resistance," defined as a form of popular contention in which those involved "frame their claims with reference to protections implied in ideologies [or laws] or conferred by policymakers" (O'Brien 1996, p. 33; O'Brien and Li 2006).[18]

Claim-Making in Practice

Here, we describe the work of citizen claimants across our country-issue cases. Both the practices and the targets of claim-making vary given the nature of citizens' grievances, as well as the institutional frameworks in which they

---

[16] See, in addition, Dunning (2009); Krishna (2011); Krishna et al. (2020); Heller et al. 2023; Garay et al. (2020).

[17] Houtzager and Acharya's typology of active citizenship ranges from "community-centric" efforts (including collective self-provisioning) to "state-centric" efforts. Our notion of claim-making focuses solely on the later: state-targeted attempts to negotiate access to entitlements.

[18] We distinguish claim-making from rightful resistance in that we do not hold that claimants necessarily seek to challenge, curb, or exploit those in power – although some may. We also see claim-making as varying in its degree of contention. Claim-making can be, and often is, bureaucratic or routine in nature.

operate. Our aim is to highlight variation across different rights arenas and settings, but also to show what is common between them.

Claiming the Right to Health in Colombia

In 1991, Colombia adopted a new constitution that sought to establish "social democratic rule of law," and which recognized a range of social and economic rights. Concurrently, Colombia established an autonomous Constitutional Court, which over time has developed into one of "the most active and powerful courts in the entire region" (Brinks 2012, p. 576). Colombia subsequently witnessed significant legal mobilization by citizens seeking to bridge the gap between their expressed legal rights and their fulfillment. For example, while the 1991 Constitution formally recognized the right to health, this was little more than a paper promise for most poor Colombians who were routinely denied insurance coverage, medicines, and treatments. A 2008 Constitutional Court decision affirmed a justiciable right to health and sought to increase the ability of individuals to make health rights claims using the *acción de tutela* procedure. A portion of these tutela claims, which are filed in lower courts, are subsequently reviewed by the Colombian Constitutional Court. The tutela procedure has become the primary instrument through which Colombians make claims for health services and support to meet medical needs.

In making claims on the state for established social rights, Colombian citizens turn to the courts rather than political parties or other channels of clientelist exchange. The courts are not necessarily immune to clientelist pressures; however, the relatively low costs and simple filing process of the tutela procedure enable individuals to directly engage in judicial claim-making without requiring political intermediation. Indeed, 85 percent of the tutela claims that Taylor analyzed were made by individuals acting directly on their own behalf.

By engaging the tutela process, Colombian citizens not only seek to realize their individual claims, but have also helped (albeit unknowingly at the level of the individual) to deepen the right to health. The deluge of health-related cases has exposed judges to the inadequacies of the healthcare system, and has prompted them to reinterpret and expand the meaning of the right to health (Taylor 2020a). Both the realization and the institutionalization of the right to health thus rest, in large part, on the actions of ordinary citizens, who through their claim-making render health-related rights a routine object of engagement by the judiciary and, in turn, by the broader healthcare system.

However, the tutela has not been equally impactful across all sectors. Claim-making regarding the right to housing, for example, has been largely stymied. Absent a similar wave of housing-related cases, a parallel reinterpretation of the right to housing – akin to what occurred for the right to health – has not occurred. The right to housing thus remains relatively less institutionalized. The tutela also remains an uneven avenue for redress, even when citizens are able to advance their claims using the procedure. Some claims are denied, and even a positive decision will not always be met with compliance. It follows that those who engage the tutela process are often ambivalent about it. Many express low confidence in the process, and in the judiciary overall, and yet continue to file tutela claims in increasing numbers over time. This is in large part because of the perception that there is no alternative; citizenship practice – in particular around issues of health – has been reshaped in a way that centers the tutela as the primary linkage to the state (Taylor 2018). The tutela has therefore become embedded in citizens' legal consciousness; they engage it because they feel they must, but not because of a high expectation that it will "work."

Claiming the Right to Housing in South Africa

South Africa's 1996 Constitution is one of the most progressive in the world, recognizing a wide range of economic, social, and cultural rights. As rights recognitions have grown, so too have the state's judicial and administrative institutions, with the creation of new spaces in which citizens can claim their social and economic rights: a new Constitutional Court, a Human Rights Commission (which provides legal services), a Public Protector's (ombudsman) office, as well as local governing bodies required to solicit citizen participation. As Taylor has observed (2020a, p. 27): "These changes not only dramatically reconfigured the expressed obligations of the state to its citizens, but also opened up new avenues for claims-making." Citizens have responded in turn through legal claim-making in the courts, as well as through other forms of petitioning and protests targeted at local and city governments (Heller 2019).

While clientelism is not uncommon in South Africa (Bøttkjaer and Justesen 2021; de Kadt and Larreguy 2018), the courts and judiciary – and the Constitutional Court in particular – is largely viewed as beyond such political machinations. During the late 1990s and early 2000s, the Constitutional Court was relatively deferential to other branches of government, and by extension to the then electorally dominant African National Congress (ANC) (Fowkes 2016). Despite this, political parties have not played a central role in supporting legal claim-making; instead, nongovernmental organizations, law clinics, and private lawyers working pro bono have taken on that role. This creates space for those who are not well connected to partisan networks to engage in claim-making by turning directly to the judiciary.

The terrain for claim-making, however, is more constrained in South Africa than in Colombia. This is in part a function of the weaker institutionalization of rights in South Africa. The Constitutional Court, while visible and empowered, is not directly accessible to most ordinary South Africans, making legal claim-making a highly mediated and costly affair (Dugard 2015). Local governments also tend to be weakly institutionalized and are viewed as deeply corrupt. Further, during the Zuma administration (2009–2018), noted for its high levels of corruption, a "shadow state" emerged across levels of government, with powerful elites capturing state institutions – although notably not the courts (Chipkin et al. 2018). Thus, while South African citizens navigate an expansive formal rights arena, they do so from a distance and in a constrained fashion.

These dynamics are illustrated in the case of housing rights in South Africa. Housing is an acute need for large majorities of the Black population, who under apartheid were restricted to living in urban townships and rural "homelands." While millions of units of new housing have been built since the mid-1990s, there continues to be large backlogs. Thus, while social rights claims of all kinds – including those related to education, social security, health and water – have increased over time, housing claims predominate. They are the most common type of claim articulated to the High Court, Supreme Court of Appeal, and Constitutional Court. The Constitutional Court has been particularly receptive to housing cases, finding in a precedent-setting case in 2000 that the state's existing policy was tantamount to neglect and therefore unconstitutional.

In practice, however, the right to housing has been interpreted – both by judges and by civil society actors – primarily in the form of prohibitions against eviction, and less in terms of the obligation of the state to *provide* adequate housing. Because of this focus on eviction, those claiming the right have come predominantly from the lower classes and informal settlements. Those well-off enough to be able to purchase their own homes do not establish corrugated tin shacks on unused land or squat in abandoned buildings, and so do not face the same threat of eviction. In contrast to Colombia's healthcare claims, housing claims in South Africa are therefore largely undertaken by those in the informal sector.

As in the case of health rights in Colombia, there is a cascade effect: the more housing (and eviction) related cases the courts hear, the more inclined judges are to act on these cases, and the more inclined citizens are to make these judicial claims. However, unlike Colombia where most tutela claimants are individuals, most claimants in South Africa are collectives: for example, social movement organizations or small groups of individuals backed by an NGO. This reflects the higher costs and more complicated procedures of legal claim-making in

South Africa, where representation by a lawyer is required and where litigation can be expensive and lengthy. Claim-making in this context is thus mediated rather than direct, engaging both attorneys and an array of other actors. The mediated and professionalized nature of claim-making in South Africa has meant that rights have been more *formally* embedded (through courts, by judges, lawyers, and NGOs) than socially embedded in ordinary citizens' legal consciousness (Tait 2021; Tait and Taylor 2023).

Claiming Social Welfare in Rural India

State commitments to social rights and associated social spending have expanded in India since the 1990s (Nayar 2009; Singh 2015). These trends intensified under the United Progressive Alliance government (2004–2014) led by the Indian National Congress party, producing an "unprecedented expansion of the welfare state" alongside a "dramatic expansion and deepening of state institutions and a shift from patronage politics to citizen empowerment" (Adhikari and Heller 2022, p. 3). Undergirding this was an array of legislation codifying the right to work (National Rural Employment Guarantee Act, 2005); the Right to Education (2009); and the right to food (National Food Security Act, 2013), as well as new social policies in public health, nutrition, drinking water, housing, and more. Landmark transparency legislation in the form of the Right to Information Act (2005) created mechanisms for citizens to demand access to government records, while creating the foundation for new accountability initiatives including social audits and grievance platforms for monitoring of public programs (Veeraraghavan 2022).

The resulting landscape is one of active claim-making through a diverse array of local institutions. The particular channels employed reflect the institutional landscape. Notably, none of India's newly established social rights were "constitutionalized" in the same legally binding sense as in Colombia or South Africa. They built instead from "directives" in the Indian Constitution that established guidelines for India's states for the provision of adequate means of livelihood, social security, and a "decent" standard of living.[19] That social rights are not formally constitutionalized is reflected in a relative lack of explicitly rights-based discourse at the local levels; while citizens express high levels of demand for government services (*"suvidha"*), they rarely do so in terms of articulated rights (*"adhikaar"*) (Jayal 2013; Kruks-Wisner 2018a). It follows that few Indian citizens turn directly to the judiciary for claim-making purposes.

---

[19] These are articulated in the Constitution of India, "Fundamental Rights," Article 21 (21A), and "Directive Principles of State Policy," Articles 38–39, 41–43, 46–47.

Instead, claim-making is more administrative in nature, as citizens seek out
governing bodies and bureaucratic offices. In rural India, much of this occurs at
the level of the *Gram Panchayat* (village council). The panchayat is India's
most local elected unit as well as a nodal point for local administration, charged
with issuing official documents, overseeing maintenance of village infrastructure, and beneficiary selection for social programs. Elected members carry out
these tasks alongside appointed personnel and contractors who supervise the
implementation of public programs. The panchayats are also hosts to participatory institutions created for the purpose of citizen monitoring of – and claim-
making related to – government programs. These include the bi-annual *Gram
Sabha*, a meeting in which budgets are approved and program beneficiaries
selected; and *jan sunwai* (public hearings) in which citizens demand records
pertaining to government programs. The panchayat is, in this sense, a key site of
what Adhikari and Heller (2022, p. 10) refer to as "retail engagement" consist-
ing of "day to day negotiations and claim-making through which effective
forms of citizenship have become embedded in local institutions."

In most states, panchayat candidates are prohibited from running on party
platforms. However, informal linkages between panchayat candidates and
political parties are well documented. This means that the panchayat often
plays a hybrid role: it is both a target of claim-making and a gatekeeper to
party networks and higher levels of government. This makes the panchayat
a critical first port of call for many citizens. In rural Rajasthan, for example,
almost two-thirds (62 percent) of those surveyed by Kruks-Wisner reported
turning to panchayat members when seeking access to government programs
and services. Far fewer (22 percent) reported turning to politicians and party
workers – most of whom operate a level above the village. In urban areas,
however, this pattern is reversed. Urban local bodies are much weaker in their
powers and resources than rural panchayats, while party networks are dense and
powerful; in India's cities, claim-making is more often mediated through partisan actors (Auerbach and Kruks-Wisner 2020).

Other channels of claim-making involve direct engagement between citizens
and the public personnel that staff India's vast central, state, and local administrative structures. For citizens seeking to access this bureaucracy, the Block
Development Office is a key institution. These offices serve an average population
of about 150,000 citizens, representing a "middle layer" in the bureaucracy; they
are not "frontline" officials but nor are they high up in the bureaucratic chain.[20]
This makes them critical nodes for the distribution of government resources that
are passed down from central and state governments (Kruks-Wisner and Kumar

---

[20] An Indian administrative block is roughly equivalent to a county in the United States.

2023). In Rajasthan, about 20 percent of survey respondents reported having personally contacted these kinds of appointed administrators. Rates of citizen contact with block offices have likely increased beyond this over time, with increases in rural mobility and connectivity. In addition, a recent proliferation of grievance redressal mechanisms have created new channels through which citizens can access administrative agencies. A recent study in Bihar, for example, documents how both the nature and volume of citizen claim-making has shifted following the creation of new quasi-judicial spaces made accessible to citizens through local complaints counters, online systems, mobile apps, and panchayat-level computer kiosks (Adhikari 2023).[21]

Combating Impunity in Mexico

Unlike social and economic rights, the rights to life, security, and protection are nearly universal: these fundamental rights are enshrined in nearly every major international human rights treaty. In Mexico, these rights are guaranteed in Article 14 of the 1917 constitution. Once the right to life is violated, a distinct set of rights is activated. The UN Human Rights Commission has laid out 38 principles that specify states' responsibility for combating impunity, including guaranteeing the right to justice, truth, reparation, and non-recurrence. There have been successful efforts, led by organized victims, to inscribe these principles in Mexican law. The Victims' Law (2013) provides for reparations for victims of Mexico's war on drugs, and the 2017 General Law on Disappearance specifies the ways in which a state must investigate, immediately respond to, and document cases of disappearances. Each of these pieces of legislation has created associated bureaucracies charged with implementing laws at both the federal and state level, including the Special Committee of Victim Attention, and Search Commissions (*Comisiones de Búsqueda*). Additionally, Mexico recently underwent an extensive legal reform shifting from a written to an oral system of justice, with the aim of making the legal system more accountable and transparent.

However, these formal legal gains are stymied by Mexico's weak judicial institutions. In a recent survey, 74 percent of Mexicans expressed little or no confidence that the justice system would punish criminals.[22] This weakness was inherited from the country's extended period of one-party rule. During the 71-year administration of the Institutional Revolutionary Party (PRI), state judicial institutions were bloated with political appointees, and served more as a sponge

---

[21] Adhikari argues that the availability of grievance platforms has promoted a qualitative shift from "relational" demands based on personal or political connections to "rule-based" claims.

[22] Data from the 2019 Americas Barometer by the LAPOP Lab, www.vanderbilt.edu/lapop.

to absorb citizen demands than as a Weberian institution capable of meting out justice. Democratization in 2000 coincided with the growing power and wealth of Mexican Drug Trafficking Organizations (DTOs). President Calderón, elected in 2006, confronted growing DTO power by deploying the army to target high-level drug traffickers. The fallout from this strategy was a spike in lethal violence throughout Mexico, and the beginning of a wave of disappearances in which the victims were everyday citizens (as opposed to political actors). This created intense judicial needs among the Mexican population. As they turned to the justice system for redress for both homicides and disappearance, they found institutions ill-equipped to investigate or prosecute cases. Mexico's federal system complicated things further. Cases of disappearances are commonly filed in multiple jurisdictions, and in each jurisdiction a dizzying array of officials from different security forces and state commissions are charged with investigation – resulting in the involvement of a large number of poorly coordinated officials.

A state-sponsored national survey[23] found that in 2020, 93.3 percent of crimes went unreported. Nevertheless, many families of the disappeared do turn to the authorities in the desperate hope that they can help find their loved ones. Unlike a homicide, a disappearance is considered ongoing until the person is located; this propels many family members into sustained claim-making over the course of years. In a nationally representative survey, Gallagher (2017, 2023) found that age, gender, level of education, and income did not predict whether individuals reported that they would pursue a claim with the state, turn to an NGO, or do nothing. Likewise, an analysis of cases reported to a local human rights NGO in Monterrey found those who chose to pursue their cases by attending ongoing participatory investigations were demographically identical to those who reported a disappearance but did not pursue the claim further. The participation of people across the socioeconomic spectrum is fueled by the perception that even wealthy people are unable to advance investigations, together with the demonstrated political ability of victims' collectives to secure meetings with prosecutors and other state officials.

In the early years of the wave of disappearances (2007–2013), claim-making was often mediated by small human rights organizations and other NGOs (*asociaciones civiles*). However, the scale of the need quickly outpaced existing civil society resources, and more than a hundred self-organized "victims' collectives" have since formed. These organizations most often are informal, and may be externally visible only through their social media presence, as well as their participation in larger national coalition organizations. They are, however, powerful vehicles for victim-led claim-making; within these collectives,

---

[23] Mexico's National Institute of Geography and Statistics (INEGI) conducts an annual national victimization survey (ENVIPE, Encuesta de Victimización y Percepción sobre Seguridad) of more than 100,000 Mexican households.

family members broker participatory investigations with the state, help each other learn the ropes of the legal system, and share tactics on how to get meetings, access and analyze case files, and find allies within the state. Individuals use the collectives primarily to navigate difficult-to-access pockets of the state, but they pursue claims related to their own cases largely autonomously.

Situating Claim-Making: Forms of Distributive Politics

Reflecting on the preceding cases, we turn now to a broader theorization of claim-making, which we understand as a form of *distributive* politics: a contest over where, how, and for whom policy is implemented, law is enforced, and public commitments are actualized. Locating claim-making as a form of distributive politics allows us, conceptually, to distinguish it from other forms of participation that are focused on the formation of law and policy (Figure 1). Citizens engaged in such agenda-setting politics seek to change the content of legislation; they can do so through the ballot (electing representatives who favor their policy preferences); and/or through the barricade (mobilizing through protest to attempt to compel policy change). Such efforts to influence policy fall largely outside the purview of our study of claim-making, which demands the distributive (or "allocative") responsiveness of officials.[24] Of course, the lines between efforts to create and realize policy, and between agenda setting and allocation, are not always clear-cut. Struggles over implementation can reshape the content of policy and law and vice versa, and so distributive and agenda-setting politics can intersect. The division depicted in Figure 1 should therefore be understood in stylized fashion, with the simple aim of highlighting the allocative (or distributive) objectives of claim-making.

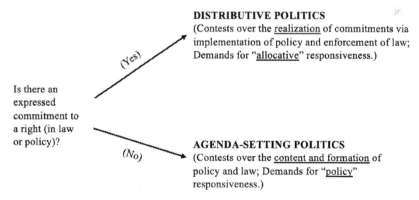

Figure 1 Claim-making is a form of distributive politics.

---

[24] Eulau and Karps (1977, p. 241) define "allocative responsiveness" as efforts by officials to ensure the "allocation of public projects" to their constituents. See also Bussell (2019).

Conceptually, we make two moves that distinguish our understanding of how citizens, as *claimants*, seek state resources from other modes of distributive politics. First, we push against a programmatic/non-programmatic binary by examining spaces where public rules of distribution play a meaningful role in shaping allocation, but which are not fully "rule-bound." Most claim-making, we argue, occurs in this middle space. Second, we depart from the assumption that the logics and incentives driving allocation are necessarily driven by electoral calculations, and that politicians and political parties are the sole or even central actors making allocative decisions.

An extensive scholarship has sought to delineate different modes of distributive politics through which public goods and resources are allocated. Landmark work by Stokes et al. (2013) distinguishes between programmatic distribution (where allocation proceeds according to publicly available rules) and non-programmatic distribution (which occurs in the absence or circumvention of public rules). Non-programmatic distribution is thought to be particularly common in "patronage democracies," where the state is a primary provider of resources that are allocated with a high degree of discretion by public officials (Chandra 2004; Bussell 2019).

However, this binary distinction between programmatic and non-programmatic politics occludes what we see as a large and important space in between the two, where public rules of allocation are applied – but irregularly so. This describes a wide array of settings where there is a *partial* influence of distributive rules, which substantively shape allocation but which are also frequently bent or ignored. It is, in our view, inaccurate to describe such settings as simply "non-programmatic," if by that term we mean either a complete absence or subversion of rules. But neither can such settings be described as programmatic, since frequent rule-bending and high levels of official discretion still mean that implementation rarely follows directly from policy.

We therefore build on but depart from the classic question posed by Stokes et al. (and taken up by Kitschelt and Wilkinson 2007; Nichter 2018; Bussell 2019; and others), who ask: Are the rules of distribution public, and do those rules shape actual distribution? Affirmative answers to those two questions, for Stokes et al., indicate programmatic conditions, while a negative answer to either one indicates non-programmatic dynamics. We instead start with the question: how *regularly* is a right realized according to de jure (formal, written) rules? By regularly we mean: how consistently are those rights realized in practice? By realization we refer to the enforcement of law, the implementation of policy, and the actualization of benefits. By de jure rules we refer to criteria that are formal (codified in law or expressed in policy directives) and written (and so publicly available). The options, depicted in stylized fashion in Figure 2, range from never, to sometimes, to always; the wide angle suggests expansive

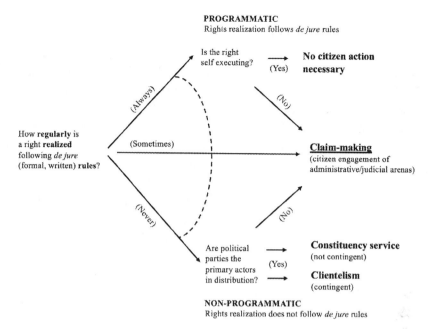

Figure 2 Modes of distributive politics.

space between the two "poles" of programmatic and non-programmatic distribution, which should be understood on a continuum rather than in discrete terms.

If the answer to this first question is "**never**" then (1) formal, written rules either do not exist or (2) they exist but are subverted or ignored. Officials, often following partisan or electoral incentives, exercise discretion in deciding when, where, and for whom to implement a policy, enforce a law, or allocate a resource. Here, rights realization does not follow de jure rules, landing us in firmly *non-programmatic* territory. In most portrayals of non-programmatic politics, politicians are conceived of as the central allocative actors. Bureaucracies, judiciaries, and other governing institutions are viewed as deeply politicized, requiring the intervention of a politician or political broker. This creates a "long route" to accountability that is mediated through partisan actors (World Bank 2004). When the party-centered modes of distribution that follow are contingent on political support, we understand this as "clientelism."[25] When not contingent, we understand this as

---

[25] We refer here both to direct modes of exchange that rest upon a quid pro quo of political support for resources, as well as to more indirect favoring of co-partisans (encompassing what Stokes et al. refer to as "partisan bias" as well as what Nichter (2018) refers to as "relational clientelism" that unfolds after elections). See also Garay et al.'s (2020) discussion of citizen perception of discretionary allocation of social benefits in Mexico.

"constituency service," following Bussell (2019) who demonstrates that politicians often act to solve citizens' problems even when they are not co-partisans.[26]

Our bodies of research, however, illuminate other pathways through which citizens can engage appointed state actors. Our second question in Figure 2, following the stylized "non-programmatic" path, is therefore whether the logics driving allocative decision-making are primarily partisan or electoral in nature. If **"yes,"** this implies that the channels through which citizens seek assistance must flow centrally through those affiliated with parties; forms of clientelism and constituency service ensue. But if the answer is **"no,"** and political parties are not the sole or even central allocative actors, this opens up the space for citizens to turn (alternatively or additionally) to administrative and judicial arenas to make claims for themselves, in ways that are not exclusively mediated by parties. This occurs, often, through direct citizen engagement with institutions designed for this express purpose: courts, for example, as well as public hearings, monitoring bodies, and other arenas for citizen oversight and redress.

Returning to the first question in Figure 2, if the answer to how regularly a right is realized is **"always,"** then (1) formal, written rules of distribution exist *and* (2) they are consistently followed. There is no discretion on the part of officials, and no gap between de jure commitments and de facto implementation. Rights realization, in other words, simply follows rules, locating us in a fully *programmatic* setting. But even in such a rule-bound context, citizens may still make claims on the state if the good or service in question is a demand-driven one that, by design, requires citizen action. One needs, for example, to apply for social security, even if it is programmatically administered. If, however, a right is "self-executing," then no action by citizens is required; the good or service will be delivered regardless of demands. Public schools, for example, will be built simply because education policy prescribes them, reflecting population parameters, if operating in a programmatic context.

If, however, the answer is **"sometimes,"** citizens find themselves in a middle space. Here, formal, written rules exist – and not just on paper. Rules, though, are applied irregularly, reflecting resource and capacity constraints as well social and political inequalities. Under these conditions, rules matter not because they consistently shape the actual responsiveness of the state, but because they (1) establish the very rights and entitlements that give shape to citizens' interests and grievances, and (2) shape the practices through which citizens engage the state. Citizens in this middle space realize that an expressed right gives them not a guarantee but a foundation for claim-making. In rural

---

[26] This, as we will discuss, can create a party-brokered pathway to claim-making.

India, for example, we observe how citizens became aware of rights and resources as they saw the state – in some places and for some people – deliver on its commitments, and so became aggrieved when they themselves did not benefit. A village resident in Rajasthan, summed up these dynamics, stating: "You would have to be blind not to see! . . . Over there they have paved roads, and the village council brought water connections to every house. Where is our road? Where is our water?"[27] In Mexico, family members with disappeared loved ones were galvanized to make demands for investigation, not because they expected the law to be uniformly applied, but because they learned through experience that investigations will only be initiated if pressure is applied. In South Africa, those living in informal settlements learned that a court order alone may not protect them from eviction attempts. One resident recounted: "We do not say, 'No, let us relax and wait for the court to decide,' because sometimes the court can . . . say, 'Leave those people, do not demolish further.' And then the next day the municipality comes and demolishes [shacks] and evicts the people."[28]

The middle space between programmatic and non-programmatic distribution is, in other words, informed by rules and rights, but driven by the unevenness with which they are enforced and fulfilled. At the same time, newly articulated or reaffirmed rights are accompanied by an expansion of mechanisms through which citizens can seek redress for failures in enforcement and fulfillment. The tutela in Colombia; the Constitutional Court in South Africa; Gram Sabhas, social audits, and grievance platforms in India; and participatory investigation units in Mexico were all designed – at least on paper – to increase citizens' access to forums in which they can "complain to the state" (Robinson 2013). Formal public commitments draw citizens into action, give shape to their interests, and create the spaces in which they articulate their complaints and demands. At the same time, claimants enter these spaces with full knowledge that rules are flexibly and partially applied, and that active pressure is required to motivate responses from officials.

Direct and Mediated Claim-Making

Claimants seek out state actors in bureaucratic or judicial agencies: administrators, appointed judges, and frontline state functionaries. Claimants' approaches to the bureaucracy or judiciary are often direct, particularly among groups of citizens who may lack the political connections necessary to pursue party- or politician-centered pathways, or who may not be members of larger movements

---

[27] Kruks-Wisner interview, Udaipur district, December 15, 2010.
[28] Taylor interview, Durban, November 29, 2017.

or associations that can mediate collective claims. The ability to *directly* navigate access to public agencies matters, since the personnel within them hold purse strings and oversee last mile implementation of policy and law. A politician can bring pressure or resources to bear, but it is at the end of the day an appointed bureaucrat, judge, or frontline government worker who does or does not take action. These unelected state actors retain at least a degree of autonomy, exercising discretion in their day-to-day interpretation of law and policy and operating in manners that are not simply reducible to partisan or electoral logics (González-Ocantos 2016; Honig 2021; Mangla 2022; Maynard-Moody and Musheno 2000; Taylor 2023b). We see this frequently across our cases where, even in highly politicized settings, politicians do not exercise full or consistent control over the day-to-day functioning of administrative or judicial agencies.

Claim-making, however, is not always a direct affair. At times, it is mediated by local actors and institutions that facilitate, gate keep, or otherwise shape citizens' access to state agencies. The particular constellation of actors varies from context to context, reflecting the local institutional environment. We draw on our cases, as well as on existing work on social and political brokerage, to offer a sketch of the range of the "institutions in the middle" (Krishna 2011) that assist citizens in seeking and gaining access to the state.

Socially Brokered Claim-Making

Social organizations serve as sites of collective identity formation (where citizens' needs are articulated and expressed), and can provide platforms for collective action (group claims). Just importantly, they can also facilitate claim-making, by connecting citizens to agents of the state, and by creating spaces in which individuals gain the knowledge, resources, and skills to make claims. As Houtzager and Acharya (2011, p. 30) note in their study of urban Latin America, local associations – in communities, neighborhoods, workplaces, and beyond – "contribute significantly to producing citizens who actively seek to negotiate their access to vital public goods and services." Krishna (2011) highlights similar intermediation in the rural Indian context, but through different channels including more informal local bodies and local leaders. From sub-Saharan Africa, to Latin America, to Central and South Asia, scholars have also noted the presence of customary institutions that can broker access to government resources and assist in motivating and coordinating citizen action (Baldwin 2016; Garay et al. 2020; Murtazashvili 2016).

Social intermediaries of all these types and more are present across our cases. In Mexico, for example, human rights NGOs together with an increasingly independent victims' movement have had broad success in pressuring state officials to officially recognize and respond to the crisis of disappearances. Individual victims, in turn, have taken advantage of these openings to build relationships with the police and prosecutors. In South Africa, major instances of legal claim-making around housing rights have been propelled by nascent, place-based movement organizations, emerging from settlements under threat of eviction, and have been supported by NGOs. In India, social movements have played a critical role in establishing the terrain for claim-making – working to both articulate and institutionalize social rights. The same movements, however, are largely absent from everyday claim-making repertoires (reported, e.g., by less than 10 percent of the sample in Rajasthan). Many more turn to local institutions including neighborhood, village, or caste associations, as well as "traditional" councils made up of caste leaders from within a village. In Rajasthan, for example, more than half of those surveyed reported engaging some kind of non-state and non-party mediating actor or group to facilitate claim-making. Even in Colombia – the case in which claim-making is the most institutionalized through the *tutela* – claimants will sometimes turn to local legal clinics and NGOs for assistance in articulating their healthcare claims.

These intermediary actors and institutions are not expressly partisan and are not involved in clientelistic, quid pro-quo exchanges. Instead, they pursue forms of "social accountability," defined as "nonelectoral yet vertical mechanisms of control of political authorities" (Peruzzotti and Smulovitz 2006, p.10). Such actors can be best understood as engaged in "social brokerage," distinguished from other forms of intermediation by "what is being asked of citizens (claim-making, rather than votes or payment) and of officials (responsiveness without the expectation of an electoral return)" (Kruks-Wisner 2022, p. 6). The rise of social accountability organizations in recent years, many of which work to "induce" bottom-up participation (Mansuri and Rao 2013), has generated new "invited" spaces (Fox 2015; Gaventa 2021). As we suggest in Section 2, the proliferation of these institutions, supported by donor interventions as well as government initiatives, may drive claim-making by pulling citizens into new spaces where they encounter the state.

Party-Brokered Claim-Making

We broadly distinguish claim-making from both clientelism and constituency service, which hinge on the intervention of politicians and political brokers. However, this distinction should not be overstated. Partisan interference in the bureaucracy as well as courts is a widely documented phenomenon (Gulzar and Pasquale 2017; Helmke 2005; Holland 2017), and partisan actors often make demands on appointed officials on behalf of citizens. A state Member of Legislative Assembly in India, for example, can ask an appointed Block Development Officer to look into delayed work payments on behalf of constituents. Similarly, a politician or political candidate in Mexico might call someone high up in the Attorney General's office to broker a meeting with a victim's family.

We refer to such practices as "party-brokered claim-making." This circuitous route flows through politicians and party workers who become "claimants" themselves by making demands on appointed officials. A growing body of scholarship explores the work of party actors beyond elections,[29] highlighting their expansive role in citizens' problem-solving repertoires (Auerbach 2019; Krishna et al. 2020; Weitz-Shapiro 2014). Just as citizens navigate a vast space between programmatic and non-programmatic politics, so too do political parties. As Hicken and Nathan (2020, p. 289) have noted, "politicians and parties rarely face a binary choice between these two extremes. Instead, many parties appear to engage in more complex hybrid appeals, simultaneously mixing various types of non-programmatic appeals with different combinations of personalism, populism, and programmatic policy." Facilitating citizen claim-making is a part of this mix.

Party-brokered claim-making is set apart from clientelism by the lack of a "transaction" (Kitschelt & Wilkinson 2007, p. 2) in which voters exchange political favor for particularistic benefits, as well as by the "non-contingent" nature of the interaction which does not rest on partisan identification. The lines between party-brokered claim-making and constituency service are necessarily blurrier, since in both cases the interaction is non-contingent. Indeed, many instances of constituency service take the form of party-brokered claim-making, as politicians work to "facilitate citizens' access to fundamental benefits and services of the state" (Bussell 2019, p. 4). For partisan actors, claim-making may indeed be electorally motivated; party workers or political elites may make demands on bureaucratic or judicial agencies (or mobilize citizens to do so) with the hope of gaining political support. But by pushing for the enforcement of law or application of policy on behalf of constituents, political actors – just like citizen claimants – are pulled into the space in between programmatic and non-programmatic politics.

The relative importance of this party-brokered path and its salience for citizens reflects the surrounding institutional environment and the strength of party networks, which vary dramatically across and within our cases. In surveys and interviews in Colombia, no tutela complainant or judge made any reference

---

[29] For a review, see Hicken and Nathan (2020).

to a political party when describing either their claim or their ruling; accessing the tutela is, by design, a direct and unmediated affair. Indeed, it is possible that institutionalization of the tutela has worked to *reduce* citizens dependence on parties; as the man in Bogotá quoted in the introduction noted, before the tutela it was "necessary to wait for a politician to be elected" but with the tutela "an individual, a single person, can file a complaint." Parties and politicians did not drive legal claim-making in South Africa either, as claims were made against the ANC-led government by their own constituents or by individuals without strong party affiliations. This is not to say that parties are absent; far from it, they are so omnipresent (in the form of the ANC) that they have become part of the tapestry of the state that citizens make claims on and against. In the case of Mexico, the abysmal track record of political parties to meaningfully advance citizens' demands for justice render them largely peripheral to claimants. Politicians are occasional background actors – using personal connections to pressure for accountability, for example by assisting in setting up meetings between victims and officials. But claimants' objective are at all times to get the attention of state personnel (investigators and the police) with jurisdiction over their loved ones' cases.

In India, parties and political brokers play a more central role in claim-making, although this varies sub-nationally – again reflecting differences in the strength of partisan networks. In urban India, party networks are dense, particularly in informal settlements (Auerbach 2019; Krishna et al. 2020). In rural India, in contrast, party networks are much thinner, and decentralized governance bodies are more developed than their urban counterparts. The result is that claim-making is more likely to be party-brokered in urban slums and to involve the direct contacting of the panchayat in villages (Auerbach and Kruks-Wisner 2020). Most rural residents of Rajasthan, for example, rarely reported meeting or even seeing higher-level (state or national) politicians, and even affiliated party workers were a relatively rare feature in rural residents' claim-making repertoires. The local panchayat, however, blurs the lines between administrative and political arenas, as a site where citizens regularly engage both elected members and appointed state personnel.

Direct and party-brokered approaches are not mutually exclusive. A mother searching for her disappeared son in Mexico, for example, described herself as "wearing different shirts" to explain how she approached different state actors at different points in time, from a presidential candidate who she hoped would connect her with the Attorney General (as a potential constituent), to the prosecutor investigating her case (directly as a legal claimant), to a social movement organization that she hoped would add pressure (socially brokered claim-making), to the state investigator's office (again as a direct claimant). In

India, rural residents similarly expressed the need to combine strategies. Recounting his efforts to access delayed pension payments, one elderly man described, "I went first to the [panchayat] meeting to make my application. But you have to go time and time again, and to so many people. I went as well to the *haath wale* [the hand people, referring to the Congress party symbol], and then back again to the panchayat."[30]

Citizens can hedge their bets by seeking assistance from appointed state actors and through parties simultaneously, or can do so in sequence (turning to a political broker if unsatisfied with a bureaucratic response, or vice versa). Politicians operating in environments where citizens can directly engage the bureaucracy may find their standing as gatekeepers challenged, potentially weakening the patron–client relationship, or lessening the need for constituency service. At the same time, however, the presence of partisan actors can influence direct claim-making, potentially giving it more bite, in settings where actors within the bureaucracy understand that there is a threat of political mediation if they do not take action on citizens' claims.

---

[30] Kruks-Wisner interview, Udaipur, Rajasthan, 2010.

2 Claim-Making Conditions

In this section, we explore the factors that give rise to claim-making in our cases, to theorize about the broader conditions that might provoke claim-making in other settings that are similarly marked by inequality and uneven state performance. We argue that claim-making is most likely to occur where the state's institutional terrain, which we understand in terms of the scope and reach of its administrative and legal apparatuses, is expanding – but *unevenly* so. This is expressed in a broadening array of commitments to citizenship rights that are inadequately realized. The state is the guarantor of rights and provider of services of central importance to citizens' lives, but citizens must actively *claim* those rights and resources in order to enjoy them.

Turning to our cases, we examine how broad shifts in political economy have produced unevenness in rights fulfillment – setting the stage for claim-making. We focus on two concurrent and seemingly paradoxical policy waves that, together, "pushed" and "pulled" citizens toward claim-making: state retrenchment on the one hand, and rights expansion on the other. Neoliberal reforms leading to cuts in social spending and a diminishment of state capacity (compounding existing inadequacies) deepened the need for public services and protections, *pushing* citizens toward claim-making. At the same time, expanding formal rights commitments – driven by constitutional and other legal reforms – broadened the scope of what citizens could claim, while also giving rise to new institutional spaces in which citizens could engage the state. This, in turn, *pulled* citizens into claim-making, as well as into new claim-making arenas. These dynamics, we show, played out in different ways across our cases, but are by no means unique to those settings. Similar "push" and "pull" factors are present in other settings – particularly those across the global south that have also experienced the countervailing dynamics of neoliberal reform and rights expansion – as well as at different historical points in time. We therefore argue, in broadest terms, that claim-making is provoked and induced by state unevenness, as citizens seek to extract goods, services, and protections from an increasingly visible but unevenly accessible state.

Rights Commitments and the Institutional Terrain of the State

Claim-making is not only state-targeted but "state induced" (Kruks-Wisner 2018a, 2018b). It is shaped by citizens' lived experiences of law and policy; that is, of whether and how well public commitments are realized. It follows that claim-making is conditioned by the institutional terrain of the state: the presence, reach, and accessibility of administrative and judicial bodies.[31] In

---

[31] We build here on the concept introduced in Kruks-Wisner (2018a), and on Heller's (2013, p. 48) related notion of the "surface area of the state."

exploring claim-making in rural India, Kruks-Wisner (2018a, p. 51) highlighted the importance of the state's "developmental" terrain: "the spaces and channels through which citizens observe and engage the state and, in particular, its welfare apparatus." We extend this notion to encompass a broader array of citizenship rights, both social and civil, focusing on what we term the *rights terrain*: the formal commitments articulated by the state, and the consistency with which citizens are able to enjoy them. Rights terrains vary cross-nationally, sub-nationally, as well as across different sectors and issue domains (the rights terrain in the domain of housing might look different than that for healthcare, for example).

We consider two key dimensions of the rights terrain. First, its de jure breadth: the scope of the entitlements, services, and protections that the state commits to provide, and the institutionalization of those commitments through the creation of formal access mechanisms. Where this de jure dimension is narrow, the state commits to only a limited array of rights, and citizens have few mechanisms through which to claim them; where broad, the array of articulated rights is expansive, accompanied by institutions for their fulfillment. These, though, are not static conditions: there is dynamic movement along the de jure dimension. When narrowing, the state backtracks, rescinds, and strips away its commitments, reducing the range of what citizens can claim. As this dimension broadens, the state formally recognizes more rights and entitlements, and its judicial and administrative footprint grows: legislation is passed; rules are written and publicized; programs are established; and public offices are formed, staffed by personnel dedicated, at least nominally, to the fulfillment of those rights.

The second dimension is the de facto uniformity or irregularity with which rights are realized. Where uniform, enforcement and implementation are rule-bound: citizens' access to entitlements and protections is equal under law and follows established criteria of eligibility. Where irregular, implementation does not necessarily follow written rules of entitlement or distribution, and citizens experience uneven access to state resources. As we showed in Section 1, however, formal rules are not without impact but serve as the foundation for claim-making. Here too, there is movement along a continuum.

The de jure and de facto dimensions combine to create different claim-making conditions, depicted in stylized fashion in Figure 3. We argue that settings are particularly ripe for claim-making where the rights terrain is *broad* (or broadening) but *irregular* – creating conditions of unevenness. A broader commitment to rights increases the scope for claim-making by enlarging both the pool of resources and the spaces in which to claim them. At the same time, the variable fulfillment of rights increases the need for claim-making since citizens' ability to secure resources does not simply follow from rules of public distribution. Claim-making, in other words, is both worthwhile and necessary.

De jure commitment to rights/entitlements

Narrow(ing) ◄┄┄┄┄┄┄┄► Broad(ening)

	Narrow(ing)	**Broad(ening)**
Uniform	**Less to claim, less need to do so** Fewer rights/resources, Regularlized provision	**More to claim, less need to do so** More expansive rights/resources, Regularized provision
Irregular	**Less to claim, more need to do so** Fewer rights/resources, Irregular provision	**More to claim, more need to do so** More expansive rights/resources, Irregular provision

De facto realization of rights/entitlements

Figure 3 Claim-making conditions.

We expect claim-making to be comparatively more limited in settings marked by both a scarcity and an abundance of realized rights commitments. Where the state's commitments are narrow, its presence as guarantor of rights or purveyor of public services is "scarce" (Nathan 2023).[32] Under these conditions, citizens are often "hard pressed to locate the state let alone make claims on it" (Kruks-Wisner 2018a, p. 220). Claim-making, in such settings, may appear a fool's errand, not worth the associated risks and costs. This can occur under conditions of both uniform and irregular rights realization: in the former, the state is rule-bound in administering a limited set of rights, while in the later, it is variable (capricious, selective) in its administration of a similarly restricted set. In either case, there is less to claim from a citizen's perspective. This does not imply that citizens are simply inactive. Citizenship practice may take other forms: citizens still vote, mobilize, and protest where the state is scarce (often to demand new and expanded rights commitments), and clientelist forms of exchange are often deeply rooted (Nathan 2023). Claim-making, moreover, may still occur, but is likely to be more limited where there are fewer articulated rights commitments, or where institutionalized fora in which to make claims on the state are absent.

---

[32] However, as Nathan (2023) has argued, "scarce" states are not necessarily or uniformly weak states. Isolated and often strategic instances of state intervention in places where the state is otherwise largely absent can have long-term effects on inequality, boosting the access and interests of certain social groups over others.

At the other end of the spectrum, where the state's commitments are more expansive and regularly enforced, resources are more readily and abundantly available. The onus on citizens to make claims is therefore reduced. Citizens, simply put, have less need to repeatedly petition the state. At both extremes, claim-making loses utility: at one end, there is less to claim, while at the other there is less need to claim. These are, of course, highly stylized portrayals; the terrain in most places and for most rights arenas is more mixed. They are, nonetheless, conceptually important conditions when theorizing what limits claim-making. We cannot – through our existing cases – probe the full range of these conditions. However, as we detail in the Conclusion, these are testable predictions, suggesting an agenda for future research.

Our focus here, drawing and extending from our country-issue cases, is on the factors that support and propel claim-making under intermediate conditions marked by relative breadth (there are rights to be secured and resources to be had) and variability in fulfillment (access is far from guaranteed). This reflects, as O'Donnell (1993) has described, varied patterns of state presence ("green areas"), effectiveness ("blue areas"), and absence ("brown areas"). The countries we study have mottled maps: green, blue, and brown exist side by side, reflecting variation in commitments, enforcement, and implementation across different sectors, rights arenas, regions, and communities. In some places and for some issues, the colors swirl together: the state is *at once* present and absent, effective and deficient. Where this occurs, citizens are both "pushed" to make claims by patterns of state neglect, and "pulled" to do so by the articulation of new law and policy and the creation of new institutional spaces.

Push and Pull: State Retrenchment and Rights Expansion

These "push and pull" dynamics can be observed across our cases and, we suggest, are also broadly visible in settings globally where the gaps between "parchment" (formal rights commitments) and "practice" (actual rights fulfillment) loom large (Gould and Barclay 2012; Kapiszewski et al. 2021). We focus on two relatively recent policy waves that, we argue, have combined to set the stage for contemporary claim-making in our cases: one (neoliberal reforms) contracting the size and reach of the state, and the other (constitutional and legal reforms) expanding states' commitments to their citizens' rights. These are by no means the only drivers of state unevenness, which can be observed around the world and at different historical moments. They are, however, particularly powerful forces that, we argue, help to explain the rise and salience of claim-making activity in our cases and beyond, particularly in the global south where many citizens have experienced the two-step dance of state retrenchment and rights expansion.

The 1980s through 2000s saw a global wave of economic and social policy reforms – pushed and adopted at the multilateral, national, and local levels – aimed at reducing the size and reach of the state through cuts in social spending, deregulation, and privatization. The result was a retrenchment of public services and a hollowing out forms of state capacity, promoting what Evans (1997, p. 85) has described as a "leaner, meaner kind of stateness." Paradoxically, these moves to reduce the role of the state in citizens' lives in fact made the state, as guarantor of rights and provider of services, even more central to the lives of the poor and marginalized, since they are the ones who could least afford to turn to market alternatives. MacLean (2011), for example, employing data from across sub-Saharan Africa, demonstrates that the rural poor were, in a climate of state retrenchment, more likely to rely on public services than more affluent urban residents who could purchase private alternatives.

The same political moment also saw a hollowing out of other arenas, specifically among institutions that have traditionally worked to mediate and represent the interests of economically and socially marginalized citizens. As Kapiszewski et al. (2021, p. 2) argue: "Corporatist structures broke down, labor movements weakened, and leftist and labor-based parties collapsed or shifted to the Right." This trend was particularly pronounced in Latin America, where, as Roberts (2022, p. 4) notes, the mid-1990s were:

> a time when every country in the region had responded to the debt crisis by initiating ambitious market reform programs ... [L]abor movements had been dramatically weakened by economic crises, market restructuring, and (in some cases) military repression, while labor-based parties were in retreat or climbing aboard the neoliberal bandwagon.

In this context, unions, parties, and social movements became less prominent as channels for citizens' interest representation (Collier and Handlin 2009), reflecting both the ideological climate and, in some settings, repressive coercion (Murillo 2000). As Dunning (2009, p. 123) has suggested, "the changing character of interest representation in the region, typified by the decline of robust union-party linkages during recent decades, may imply new constraints on political participation, [but] it may also afford opportunities for novel modes of political problem solving." These opportunities include forms of direct action, like citizen claim-making.[33]

Similar shifts propelled citizens in settings around the globe to begin to seek out new avenues of access and redress beyond parties, unions, and other classic

---

[33] See also Boulding and Holzner 2020, 2021; Kapiszewski et al. 2021.

platforms for representation (Alexander and Fernandez 2021; Baccaro and Howell 2017). These macro-level dynamics – neoliberal policy reforms and the relative decline of unions and labor-aligned parties, which emerged concurrently in some contexts but independently in others – pushed citizens toward direct claim-making within administrative and judicial arenas of the state, in particular as other avenues for interest representation seemed to run dry.

Yet, at the very same time that states seemed to retrench, a second global policy wave was unfolding, visible in dramatic *expansions* of rights recognitions in international law as well as in domestic constitutions, law, and policy-making. In 1995, The United Nations proclaimed the start of the UN Decade for Human Rights Education. The years following saw human rights discourse diffuse globally, with international human rights institutions becoming more prominent than ever before (Moyn 2010). This discourse manifested itself in domestic institutions using rights language to guarantee citizens' expanded civil, political, and social protections. A spate of legislation guaranteeing new rights (e.g., recognizing the rights of women to full protection of the law; of indigenous groups to collective land rights; of all citizens to healthcare, housing, food, and water) was passed and many of those same rights were codified in domestic constitutions – a trend referred to as social constitutionalism.

While rights recognitions had long been part of constitutionalism, this period saw a significant shift in the choice by states to "add *social* rights to existing documents or replace their old constitutions with more *rights-rich* texts" (Brinks et al. 2015, p. 293, emphasis added). In what Kapiszewski et al. (2021) describe as an "inclusionary turn," governments employed legislation and constitutional reforms to expand protections for groups that had long been marginalized. In some settings, these rights expansions served to reconfigure existing social assistance and redistributive regimes. Whereas prior models of welfare provision may have rested on kinship, union membership, or employment status, access to social welfare goods became, at least on paper, a matter of *rights* (Seekings 2005).

New and reaffirmed rights commitments – in the areas of social welfare and human rights alike – were in many cases accompanied by institutional changes that gave rise to new spaces where citizens could make claims on the state. This occurred, often, through institutions designed expressly for this purpose; courts, for example, as well as public hearings, grievance platforms, monitoring institutions, and other mechanisms for public oversight. Many of these new avenues for accessing the state emerged in response to calls for greater citizen inclusion in governance alongside the global spread of decentralization reforms.

These concurrent policy waves are seemingly at odds: neoliberal retrenchment curtails the distributive capacity of state, while broadening rights guarantees expands the state's commitments, as does the growth of its administrative footprint. Neoliberalism would seem to undercut or limit rights expansion, and vice versa. Scheppele (2013, p. 550) argues that these dynamics have led to the emergence of "Frankenstates," which are "composed from various perfectly reasonable pieces, [but their] monstrous quality comes from the horrible way that those pieces interact when stitched together." Rather than working together, these features undermine one another. Some have suggested that this is intentional. Merino (2020), for example, argues that the discourse of rights is "cheap talk," giving cover to states that act to limit the effectiveness of those rights. Brinks et al. (2015, p. 294) suggest a somewhat less cynical thesis–antithesis relationship between rights expansion on the one hand and neoliberalism on the other, arguing that "a series of events – the dismantling of ... welfare states, the end of the Cold War and the incorporation of the 'Second World's' concern for welfare rights ... and general disillusionment with neoliberal market prescriptions ... – seemed to call for a new approach to social democratic politics." In this view, social constitutionalism serves as a response, and a possible antidote, to neoliberal retrenchment.

Whether we view the combination of state retrenchment and rights expansion as paradoxical happenstance, cynical creation, or counter movements, these two waves work with and against each other to produce and/or exacerbate uneven conditions: expansive rights regimes and more inclusionary policies and institutions on the one hand, and limited implementation capacity on the other. The simultaneous "push" of neoliberal reforms and "pull" of expanding rights have created new need, spaces, and momentum for state-targeted claim-making. The relative decline of parties, unions, and other vehicles for interest representation propel citizens into more direct forms of seeking rights fulfillment, while an expansion of governance institutions, many designed to accompany new rights, invite citizens into new claim-making spaces and practices. We illustrate these dynamics across our four cases.

Push and Pull in Colombia

The 1991 Colombian Constitution set out a social constitutionalist vision at the same time that the Gaviria administration pursued neoliberal economic policy. This meant that Colombia was simultaneously committing itself to noninterference in the market *and* the state-led protection of social rights. Indeed, as Uprimny Yepes (2006) notes, "the government's neoliberal policies soon converted the [Constitutional Court] into practically the only body disposed to and capable of implementing the Constitution's progressive content." One of the hallmarks of social constitutionalism, as it is practiced in Colombia and elsewhere, is that it assigns a central role to judicial institutions in adjudicating claims to social goods, rather than to political parties, legislative bodies, or state service agencies. This turn to judicial power is one that is (perhaps) unintentionally consistent with certain aspects of neoliberal thought, with its concern for individuals and disdain for group-based politics (Harvey 2007). In Colombia, these two forces worked together to create a landscape defined by broad rights promises and uneven rights realizations. It also created the impetus for individual claim-making through the courts, as facilitated by the tutela procedure (described in Section 1).

The gap between rights and realization was particularly acute with respect to healthcare. A legal reform ("Law 100") in 1993 radically redesigned the healthcare system and, over time, served to dramatically expand formal access. Whereas in 1995, only about 25 percent of the population was formally included in the healthcare system (covered by public, private, or mixed insurance providers), by 2016 that number jumped to 95 percent of the population (Lamprea 2015; Lamprea and García 2016). The ideas behind this healthcare reform married the neoliberal commitment to market-oriented provision of goods with the rights commitments articulated in the 1991 Constitution. Private entities would administer insurance coverage and healthcare services, and individual contributions would help make the system fiscally responsible, but in accordance with a government-designed health plan. A parallel system would exist for those who could not afford to pay into the contributory system. As Taylor has written (2020a, p. 1337): "the massive yet uneven expansion of the healthcare system generated many potential grievances, as citizens gained access in theory (if not delivery in practice) to more and more services and developed a greater sense of entitlement to those services." In response, citizens filed tutela claims to bridge the gap between their rights on paper and the actual access to care they experienced. In so doing, they brought healthcare into the realm of the courts.

Push and Pull in South Africa

In South Africa during the struggle against apartheid, members of the ANC developed a sense of not only race but also class consciousness (Suttner 2012), which was expressed in calls for social and economic rights. In 1990, the ANC issued its "Bill of Rights for a New South Africa," which proclaimed:

> We do not want freedom without bread, nor do we want bread without freedom. We want freedom, and we want bread . . . Our approach has been to identify certain needs as being so basic as to constitute the foundation of human rights claims, namely, the rights to nutrition, education, health, shelter, employment and a minimum income (pp. vii–viii).

This view reflects core tenets of social constitutionalism, later embodied after the end of apartheid in the 1996 Final Constitution and the newly created Constitutional Court. Yet, at the same time, the international system, and therefore South Africa's sources of political and economic support, shifted. The Soviet Union fell, and the Washington Consensus on neoliberalism came to dominate international institutions including those directing the flow of much needed aid and capital. Even so, the ANC pushed against the institutions that defined global neoliberal commitments, for example by rejecting loan offers from the International Monetary Fund even in the face of significant budgetary constraints (Boughton 2012). Thus, while neoliberal retrenchment was not formally imposed within South Africa, the global dominance of neoliberalism nonetheless limited the options – and funding – available to the government as it sought to fundamentally reorient the state and its commitments to its citizens.

A key part of the reorientation of the South African state was to provide access to social welfare goods, notably among them housing. Access to housing took on special significance considering the history of apartheid, which systematically restricted access to housing and land along racial lines. In the first few years of majority rule, the ANC government enacted its Reconstruction and Development Program (RDP). Over the next decade, more than four million new homes were built and housing subsidies offered through the RDP and subsequent programs. Still, the South African government faced numerous economic, political, and infrastructural challenges, and by 2016, the number of informal settlements in the country had increased and housing backlogs were almost twice as long as they were in 1994.[34] As was the case with health in Colombia, the tension between rights promises and economic realities has meant uneven access to housing in South Africa. Citizens – notably those organized within informal settlements – have met this unevenness head on in the courts.

Push and Pull in India

India, like Colombia and South Africa, also experienced concurrent waves of neoliberal reform and rights expansion. The 1990s was a moment of dramatic political and economic change, marking the end of Congress party rule.[35] The 1990s were also a time of economic liberalization, starting with a package of structural adjustment reforms in 1991 promising trade and financial

---

[34] National Department of Human Settlements, "Annual Performance Plan" (2017), 15.

[35] The Indian National Congress was the leading political organization of the Indian Independence movement. Following Independence, it became the dominant political party in most states, leading the central government almost consecutively for more than forty years from 1947 to 1989.

liberalization, privatization of state-owned enterprises, and other actions to secure the support of the International Monetary Fund. And yet, at the same moment, central and state governments began to *increase* social sector programming and spending. As Jayal (2013, p. 164) has observed, formal commitments to social rights "gained momentum in a policy environment that emphasized state withdrawal from public provisioning." This is reflected in what Nayar (2009) has called the "myth of the shrinking state." Government spending on education and health more than doubled in real terms from the late 1970s to the mid-2000s, while spending on social security quadrupled.

These trends accelerated in the 2000s with a wave of rights-based social legislation, reflecting what Mooij and Dev (2004, p. 100) refer to as a shift from a "basic needs" approach to a "human development" approach couched in language of "economic and social rights." These rights, as noted in Section 1, were not "constitutionalized" in the same manner as in Colombia and South Africa, but were nonetheless written into law in the form of national and state legislation, accompanied by a mushrooming of social programs.[36] These many programs, while mandated at the central and state levels, were locally implemented – requiring a larger role for local bureaucrats as well as the *Gram Panchayat*. Thus, at the same time that social policies expanded, so too did the state's *local* penetration.

As Gupta (2012, p. 23) writes, "one could hardly accuse the [Indian] state of inaction toward the poor: it would be difficult to imagine a more extensive set of development interventions in the fields of nutrition, health, education, housing, employment, sanitation, and so forth than those found in India." And yet, for most Indian citizens, the lived gap between policy and implementation remains a yawning one, reflecting constrained state capacity (Pritchett 2009), bureaucratic overload (Dasgupta and Kapur 2020), and rampant graft (Sukhtankar 2017). The result, as Gupta (Op. cit. p. 14) writes, is a local administrative setting "shot through with contingency and barely controlled chaos." Under these conditions, rural citizens experience the unevenness of the state, which is "both present and absent, visible and elusive, and critical and capricious in the lives and livelihoods of the poor" (Kruks-Wisner 2018a, p. 63).

---

[36] Most notable among these for its scope and budget is the National Rural Employment Guarantee Scheme, which in 2010 accounted for 3.6 percent of all government expenditures and 0.5 percent of total Indian GDP (Sukhtankar 2017). The Targeted Public Distribution System, which distributes food and non-food items to those living below the poverty line, covers more than 23 percent of Indian households. Other programs include: Sarva Shiksha Abhiyan (the "Education for All Campaign"), the National Rural Health Mission, the Midday Meals Scheme for schools; Indira Awaas Yojana (for rural housing); and the Indira Gandhi National Old Age Pension Scheme.

Push and Pull in Mexico

Mexico transitioned from a semi-authoritarian state following seventy-one years of one-party rule to a democracy with competitive multi-party elections in 2000. At the same time, Mexico battled similar economic problems as in our other cases, though perhaps more severely because of its dependence on oil as a primary export. After world oil prices collapsed in the early 1980s, Mexico faced a debt crisis and was forced to adopt neoliberal austerity measures in order to access international capital. Mexico further embraced neoliberalism in 1994 when it entered the North American Free Trade Agreement (NAFTA).

Mexicans hoped for a new era of freedom, political participation, and equality following democratization in 2000. Instead, inequality continued to deepen following NAFTA's devastating impact on much of the agricultural sector, and it soon became apparent that weak state capacity, particularly within the police and judiciary, made it impossible for Mexico to confront the growing power of DTOs or to deter crime. Long-standing rent-seeking arrangements between the state and cartels were upended as the coercive capacity of DTOs soared and PRI-backed security forces withered. The incapacitated judicial system – especially at the state level – prevented it from intervening effectively as the Mexican government lost its monopoly on the use of force.

The federal government's response, in part, was to double down on formal rights guarantees. In 2011, Mexico amended its constitution to fully incorporate international human rights standards in their national legal landscape. A month later, Mexico's Supreme Court decided to comply with a broad-reaching Inter-American Court ruling in the 1974 case of the enforced disappearance of activist Rosendo Radilla. Under this ruling, military jurisdiction would be limited and Mexican judges would be required to ensure domestic legislation was compatible with the American Convention on Human Rights. In short, faced with a deepening security crisis, Mexico has ramped up its promises of justice. Unsurprisingly, this only widened the gap between formally guaranteed rights and their fulfillment.

Claim-making under Uneven Conditions

How do these push–pull dynamics play out, to give rise and shape to claim-making? As MacLean (2011, p. 1257) has argued, the "gap between popular expectations and actual policy implementation on the ground" plays a critical role in shaping citizen–state relations. Roberts (2021, p. 534) suggests that this "parchment-practice" gap exists "in part because citizens – especially those of lower social status – are too poorly organized to exercise or claim them." We argue, however, that such gaps can catalyze claim-making, as citizens mobilize to try to realize the parchment promises of the state.

To illustrate, we turn again to our country-issue cases, all of which are marked by an uneven rights terrain. Colombia, South Africa, India, and Mexico are all low- or middle-income democracies that express formal commitments to an expansive array of citizenship rights. However, as we have described, citizens' enjoyment of those rights remains variable and constrained. In what follows, we demonstrate how the de jure articulation of rights in each case has created a judicial and bureaucratic architecture for claim-making. This expansion of the state's rights apparatus works in combination with citizens' uneven experiences of rights fulfillment to provoke claim-making.

We describe three channels through which citizens' encounters with a broad but uneven rights terrain are converted into claim-making action. First, it can be a matter of *comparative grievance* (Kruks-Wisner 2018a), provoked by the observation of rights fulfilled in other places or for other people. Claim-making, in this sense, is set in motion by state provision, which can spark new interests or reinforce an existing sense of need. Claim-making becomes a viable strategy when citizens observe others successfully engaging and making demands on the state. Second, claim-making can occur when citizens sense that *there is no alternative* (Taylor 2018); there is, in this view, simply no other strategy available to gain access to necessary goods and services. Claim-making thus becomes implanted in citizens' legal consciousness – it is simply what one has to do. Third, and related, the *nature of the grievance*, when grave and critical, can compel claim-making despite myriad reasons to give up on seeking access or redress (Gallagher 2022); claim-making, here, is a matter of life and death and so not a choice.

We see evidence of all of these channels, as well as their interactions, across our cases. By observing the actions of the state, as well as the behavior of other citizens, potential claimants come to see issues in their lives as problems they might be able to do something about, and not just an unfortunate reality. They see that others have dealt with similar problems and that some have gained recognition from the state or even a resolution. And they see that redress will not happen unless they agitate for it, by making claims.

In India, for example, the expanding array of goods and services offered on paper have raised citizens' expectations about what the state can and should provide. Much of this is driven by exposure; seeing services delivered and rights upheld for others makes one's own lack of fulfillment unacceptable, and so makes those rights subjects of claim-making (Kruks-Wisner 2018a, 2018b). A sense of comparative grievance unfolds as "as knowledge of public resources expands faster than one's own access to goods and services" (Kruks-Wisner 2018a, p. 193). It also reflects citizens' awareness of the unequal social structures in which they are embedded. A Scheduled Tribe (ST) man in Rajasthan, for example, expressed this in a heated exchange with an "upper" or general caste (GC) man in his village:

GC Man: This village has everything. Roads, drinking water, schools. There is so much development!

ST Man: Those facilities are just for rich people. Even if you have to go to the doctor you have to wait!

GC Man: Just compare this village to other places and you will understand how much you have here.

ST Man: *I do compare*! That's how I know how many facilities there are, and how little we [in the tribal hamlet] have. You might live your whole life in some far off *basti* [hamlet] and never know what all schemes you *mukhya* [main] people are getting here. But every day I am coming here and seeing your riches.[37]

As this exchange reveals, the act of comparison not only provides information about public services but also creates new grievances as citizens' expectations of the state expand.

With respect to healthcare in Colombia and housing in South Africa, the view that there is no alternative to claim-making has become prominent. Whether or not citizens originally thought of their struggles for healthcare or housing as related to legal rights, these issues have now been pushed into the formal legal sphere. As detailed earlier, Colombian citizens began early on to experiment with filing tutela claims to challenge denials of access to treatments, medications, and procedures. Finding that the courts were willing to accept these claims, citizens began to file more of them. Over time, citizens came to see filing a tutela claim as part and parcel of how one seeks healthcare services. Citizens are not confident that engaging the tutela procedure will always lead to the outcomes they want, but they see filing a tutela as simply what one has to do. A resident of Bogotá, for example, summed up this perspective, recounting:

My sister has a very complicated medical problem and has to take medications ... She had to file a tutela claim for the [insurance company] to cover them ... . There are cases in which, unfortunately, if you think about

---

[37] Conversation observed during author interview, Bargaon block, Udaipur district, December 15, 2010. Replicated from Kruks-Wisner (2018a).

it, it should not be a tutela claim. There should be an established process for each thing, but the tutela has become the thing that one has to use to gain access to citizenship services.[38]

In South Africa, the view that there is no viable alternative to claim-making stems directly from the constitutional text, which stipulates that evictions cannot proceed without a court order, and so creates the perception that legal claims must be at least part of any strategy to protect one's housing rights. Citizens do not have much choice in whether or not to engage the courts; legal notice is part of the formal eviction process, and that notice must be challenged in court, if it is to be challenged.

In Mexico in the case of disappearances, there is a related sense that while claim-making might not be the *only* option, it is an obvious and necessary step among many. The nature of disappearances – that it is an ongoing crime, and the possibility that the person could be alive and suffering – compels urgent and desperate action by their loved ones. This often means a scattershot approach, with victims filing claims in all of the possibly relevant bodies (with local, state, and national police, prosecutors, and human rights offices). As victims file these claims, they learn about what is effective, who is responsive, and about the strategies of others in the same situation. Those who continue to make claims become, over time, increasingly strategic in navigating and making demands on the state. Many victims' families have begun to utilize participatory investigations (*mesas de trabajo*, described earlier). Since establishing these regular meetings with officials is costly (requiring considerable pressure, mobilization, and confrontational tactics), claim-makers are often reluctant to give up on them – even when they fall short of their promises. They see that the fate of cases for which there is no participatory investigation are virtually guaranteed to be forgotten and unsolved. By participating in *mesas de trabajo*, in contrast, there is some slim hope that by continuing to engage the state they will make some progress.

Minding the Gap: Variation in Claim-Making

In all the preceding examples, claim-making is provoked by needs but also by citizens' expectations, and by the extent to which various rights and practices have become embedded in their legal consciousness. And yet, the same examples also highlight the varied nature of claim-making that unfolds under different institutional settings and with regard to different grievances. Here, we consider how the nature of different "de jure–de facto" gaps provokes claim-making of different kinds.

---

[38] Taylor interview, Bogotá, March 2017, 44.

Figure 4 presents a stylized visualization of where our country-issue cases fall in terms of the extent of the gap in rights realization. In each case, a formal expansion of or recommitment to citizenship rights, accompanied by the development of new institutions for fulfillment and redress, increased the terrain for claim-making. In all cases, there is a gap; none are settings with fully rule-bound implementation and enforcement.

The case of healthcare rights in Colombia represents the smallest gap. The right to health is codified in the Colombian constitution, accompanied by new legal institutions (notably the *acción de tutela*) that allow ordinary citizens to directly and individually engage the judiciary. Over time, through practice and repeated exposure, the right to health has become deeply embedded in both citizens' and judges' imaginations, and claim-making for healthcare has become ubiquitous. Even so, an access gap remains. The right to health is not simply given; citizens must *claim* it and must engage the tutela to do so. Some even have to file contempt orders (*incidentes de desacato*) to ensure compliance with the original tutela decision.

Housing rights in South Africa and welfare rights in India are mixed cases, although for different reasons. In South Africa, the right to housing is, like the right to health in Colombia, codified in constitutional law. But the formal processes for claiming the right to housing are more costly and mediated. There is no access mechanism remotely equivalent to the *acción de tutela*. Engaging the legal system can take years, and requires legal representation and other costly measures. The interpretation of the right to housing in South Africa is also thinner than that of the right to health in Colombia, as courts and civil society actors alike have interpreted the right in negative terms of freedom from eviction. The gap between formal housing rights and their realization is thus a yawning one, in large part reflecting the persistence of stark racial, class, and geographic inequalities. And so, while the rights promises of the South African state are roughly similar to those of Colombia, the failures of local fulfillment and provision are deeper.

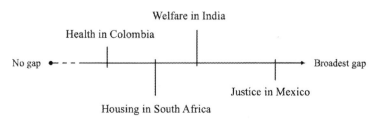

Figure 4 Gap between rights commitments and realization.

In India, welfare rights commitments (to work, to income support, to social assistance) have proliferated but are more thinly institutionalized, lacking the constitutional bite and backing of powerful courts as in South Africa and Colombia. The National Rural Employment Guarantee, for example, established a legal right to work for rural residents. But workers who are underpaid, paid late, or not paid at all have come to learn that they must make claims on the state (Jenkins and Manor 2017; Veeraraghavan 2022). Both the notion of a right to work (i.e., the expectation that the government should provide employment) and a set of claim-making practices (demanding to see muster rolls that log workers hours, contacting local contractors and panchayat officials, and participating in social audits) have become increasingly embedded in citizens' legal and political consciousness as a regular and necessary part of how they interact with the state.

The de jure–de facto gap is most extensive in the case of the right to truth and justice in Mexico. As the crisis in disappearances has deepened, Mexico's government has leaned into institutional reforms and formal access mechanisms to provide redress to victims and their families. As an international human rights lawyer told Gallagher in 2021, "the legislation is nearly perfect—the challenge is to implement it." While some policies function some of the time (financial assistance to victims, for example), the overwhelming majority of family members still don't know where their loved ones are, and there are few investigations into, much less prosecution of, those responsible. This is less a matter of uneven enforcement of law, and more a matter of *non*enforcement (i.e., the non-realization, rather than variable realization, of rights). And still, claim-making persists in the face of nonenforcement, driven by grave necessity.

To summarize, the uneven conditions of the rights terrain vary across countries, sub-nationally, and across different types of rights. The key drivers of this variation are the extent to which a given right, in a given setting, is not only articulated but also institutionalized through formal access mechanisms; as well as the ways in which citizens and state actors come to understand the right in question, and its embeddedness in their legal consciousness and practice. When the gap between promises and fulfillment is greatest, claim-makers may face more complex institutional environments, requiring more frequent claims on the state. Claim-making occurs across all these settings, but these factors shape the forms it takes.

3 Claim-Making Consequences

The previous two sections defined claim-making and theorized the conditions under which it is likely to emerge: in uneven settings where state commitments to rights are both broad and variable. In this section, we turn to the impact of claim-making. How does claim-making shape citizens' access to rights, entitlements, and protections? How does citizens' claim-making impact the state? What do these patterns of citizen (dis)engagement and government (un)responsiveness mean for citizen–state relations?

Claim-making can prompt both material changes in terms of who has access to goods or services, as well as qualitative shifts in how state institutions and actors respond to citizen demands. In what follows, we first discuss the impact of claims fulfilled (or denied) on the people that make them. We illustrate how claim-making meaningfully affects citizens' lives, visible in cases resolved, rights upheld, goods delivered, and benefits received. We also discuss the impact of claims that are stymied or ignored, and the intersection of claim-making and inequality. We then reflect on the larger implications of claim-making for patterns of citizen–state engagement, including possibilities for positive, negative, and "ambivalent" feedback effects.

Bridging the Gap: Material and Human Consequences of Claim-Making

When claim-making is successful, its impact is palpable: de jure commitments become de facto, policy is implemented, and rights are realized. Depending on the nature of the claim being made, the outcomes can be dramatic or seemingly mundane, impacting individuals, small groups, or larger collectives. A community gains access to drinking water, an individual forces the government to pay a hospital bill, a neighborhood forestalls evictions, a family uncovers the fate of a disappeared loved one. In other instances, the outcomes of claim-making are less clean cut; rights may be only partially fulfilled or a problem only partially resolved, requiring continued efforts by citizens over time. In still other instances, claim-making fails, as citizens meet with unresponsive – or worse – punitive reactions from officials.

In what follows, we describe how claim-making has begun to bridge the gap between states' promises and practices, while also highlighting the incomplete and varied nature of these impacts. Our accounts are necessarily brief given space constraints,[39] but serve to demonstrate that there have been incremental but significant changes in access to goods, services, or protections. It is difficult to causally attribute these gains singularly to

---

[39] See our books for more detail (Gallagher 2022; Kruks-Wisner 2018a; Taylor 2023a).

claim-making.[40] Our efforts to highlight the material impacts of claim-making should therefore be treated as a first approximation; future research should further catalog and quantify the material consequences of claim-making across space and over time.

Effective Healthcare Coverage in Colombia

Since the early 1990s, more and more Colombians have gained formal (paper) access to healthcare. The Law 100 reforms of 1993, which created a managed competition-style system with a contributory and a subsidized healthcare scheme, drove this expansion in formal coverage to almost 95 percent of the population by 2016 (Lamprea and García 2016). This expansion alone is striking. Prior to these reforms, regular access to quality healthcare was unimaginable for most Colombians. With the constitutionalized right to health and subsequent reforms, that access became a legal guarantee. But claim-making has been necessary to convert that right into reality. The tutela has emerged as the central mechanism for citizens to demand fulfillment of the right to health, if and when they are denied some treatment or procedure. The result is a dramatic expansion in "effective" (or substantive) health coverage. Colombia's effective coverage index, which assesses the extent to which "people [can] receiv[e] the health services they need, of high quality, without experiencing financial hardship," increased from 55.7 in 1990 to 74.4 in 2019, out of a maximum of 100 (Lozano et al. 2020). This change indicates not only that citizens' health improved but also that healthcare services improved in quality and cost.

It is difficult to isolate the independent effect of claim-making through the tutela on health outcomes overall. Much has changed, from the Law 100 reforms, to the official end of the decades-long armed conflict, to the development of new medicines and medical techniques. Even so, we can reasonably make inferences about the consequences of tutela claims for individual claimants. In 2019, someone filed a tutela claim approximately every 51 seconds, with more than 207,000 of those claims involving the right to health; 80 percent of these health claims were decided in favor of the applicant (Defensoría del Pueblo 2020).[41] Another study examining tutela claims in 2014 estimated a compliance rate of 72 percent (Carlin et al. 2022). If we assume that this rate has remained steady since 2014, we can then estimate that roughly 120,000 of the health claims

---

[40] We are constrained not least because of the absence of clear counterfactuals (what would have happened without claim-making?), as well as by the complex "supply side" factors (state [in] capacity, technocratic and political decision making, bureaucratic norms) that also shape citizens' access to goods, services, and protections.

[41] The year 2019 marks the most recent year for which data are available and not impacted by the coronavirus pandemic.

decided in favor of applicants in 2019 would have resulted in tangible gains – granting claimants access to necessary medications, procedures, and insurance coverage that otherwise would have remained little more than paper promises.

Limiting Evictions in South Africa

One legacy of apartheid was the appalling state of housing access. The combination of a lack of security of tenure, forced relocation to "homelands," limited housing stock for families, and the rise of dilapidated hostels and dormitories for individual workers, meant that many Black South Africans lived in inadequate housing as majority rule began. With that in mind, the ANC-led government has sought to provide freestanding housing units and to "upgrade" informal settlements by either demolishing them and building new housing or by providing in situ developments over time (Del Mistro and Hensher 2009). Between 1994 and 2018, the government reports having built 3.2 million new housing units.[42] In 2019, the portion of the national population living in formal dwellings reached 84 percent, compared to 65 percent in 1996, while 11 percent lived in informal housing in 2019, down from 16 percent in 1996.[43] In urban areas, though, the percentage living in informal housing is estimated to be around 20 percent (SERI 2020).

South Africa's courts, during this same time period, have begun to actively uphold the right to housing through landmark cases prohibiting evictions that would result in homelessness. It is again difficult to demonstrate the direct impact of claim-making by citizens. But legal claims – often by neighborhood collectives supported by NGOs or movement organizations – have clearly limited the ways in which both public and private actors can attempt to evict both lawful and "unlawful occupiers" of abandoned land. Further, provincial and municipal governments – as a direct result of legal claim-making – have also begun to develop plans for the provision of temporary alternative accommodation when evictions would lead to homelessness (SERI 2020). The extent to which such accommodation is both adequate and actually provided remains to be seen. Housing rights in South Africa thus remain only partially realized; they are nonetheless a matter of ongoing citizen contestation and claim-making.

Accessing Welfare Goods and Services in India

The welfare goods and services at stake in the Indian context – ranging from income support, to social services, to basic infrastructure such as drinking water – carry real consequences for human welfare. From the 1990s to late

---

[42] Statistics SA, as cited in BBC (2019).   [43] Statistics SA (2016) and (2019).

2000s, life expectancy in India rose from 58 to 65, while infant mortality rates fell from 81 to 47 per 1000 live births (Drèze and Sen 2013). Rajasthan in particular saw pronounced gains in the same period, between 1991 and 2001; it enjoyed the single largest increase among states in literacy since independence, rising from 39 percent to just above 60 percent (Singh 2015). Rajasthan also recorded advances in health, with steep declines in infant mortality beginning in the 1990s. These national- and state-level trends, however, mask local variation across communities and within social groups in real access to goods and services. As Banerjee (2004, p. 3) has observed, local access to public resources is not simply a matter of legal entitlement but rather of who can "extract them from the political system."

While it is not possible to make clear causal attributions between claim-making and aggregate welfare gains, there is a significant correlation between making claims and access to publicly provided welfare goods. This is visible in the survey data from Rajasthan, where the incidence of claim-making is associated with a 3.5 percent rise on an index of services received (Kruks-Wisner 2018). More striking, however, is how citizens *themselves* assess claim-making. When asked whether their actions were effective at solving the problems at hand, 68 percent responded in the affirmative. Notably, most stated that their efforts were "somewhat" (as opposed to "very") effective, indicating the fraught nature of claim-making, which does not guarantee either access or the seamless resolution of problems. As Kruks-Wisner has noted (2018a, p. 8), claim-making may be best understood as an "often *necessary* but also often *insufficient* condition: citizen voice is rarely enough alone to ensure the delivery of public resources, but it can play a critical role in influencing their provision."

Poking Holes in the Blanket of Impunity in Mexico

There have been more than 100,000 disappearances in Mexico since 2006, according to the government's own data. In cases without active claim-making by victims, the norm is that not a single investigative action is taken after a disappearance is reported. The impunity rate – the denial of the rights to truth, justice, reparations, and non-repetition – therefore approaches 100 percent. In this context of widespread and routinized institutional inaction, claim-making by the families of victims of disappearance has been one of the only strategies that has proven effective in moving the needle on impunity.

Precise evaluations of the national impact of claim-making is complicated by fragmented and opaque state-supplied data. To address these data problems, Gallagher (2017, 2023) turned to embedded work with a local human rights NGO located in Nuevo León, where she participated in the *mesas de trabajo*, created a database for the NGO from their case files, interviewed state investigators, and accompanied NGO lawyers. Through this work, she found that the NGO had documented the disappearance of 269 people between 2009 and 2012, the peak years of violence and disappearances in Nuevo León. In these 269 cases of disappearances, 37 had at least one indicted perpetrator, and 12 people were found guilty for a crime associated with the disappearance (some of those found guilty were responsible for multiple disappearances). In 21 percent of cases, the disappeared person was located or identified – though most of those people (89 percent) were deceased and identified through DNA. While these outcomes paint a picture of tenacious impunity, they also indicate the modest yet critical impact of claim-making. For the families of the 37 people for whom there was an indictment, and for those of the 21 percent who were located or identified, these outcomes represent dramatic advances.

Feedback Effects: Claim-Making and Citizen–State Relations Over Time

Claim-making, as illustrated in Section 2, is often repeated and iterative in nature. This is true not only in the short term and at the individual level, but also when we consider how claim-making affects broad patterns of citizen–state engagement. The idea that the process of policy implementation can dynamically shape the context in which citizens make claims is not new. The notion of feedback loops has long been used by political scientists as a lens through which to understand the ways in which "policies, once created, reshape politics" (Mettler and Sorelle 2018). As Pierson (1993, p. 595) notes, the importance of feedback processes has become evident as "[i]ncreasing government activity [has] made it harder to deny that public policies [are] not only outputs of but important inputs into the political process, often dramatically re-shaping social, economic, and political conditions." Scholars of feedback effects have demonstrated various ways in which interactions with state actors and programs can impact citizens. While these interactions shape access to material resources, they can also work to change incentive structures, as well as citizens' interests and perceptions of the state. This, in turn, can shape whether and how citizens make claims. Campbell (2012, p. 342) summarizes:

> How generous benefits are, whether they are earned, how visible the govern-
> ment role is, how proximate other beneficiaries are, how long program
> membership lasts, and how programs are administered affect both whether
> programs augment or undercut individuals' politically relevant resources and
> what kind of messages individuals receive about the legitimacy of their claim
> to benefits and their worth to society.

Feedback effects can lead to both politicization and depoliticization of different issues. On the one hand, citizens may feel aggrieved, empowered, or otherwise compelled to take action. On the other hand, citizen–state interactions can "render previously viable alternatives implausible" and lead to "non-decisions," effectively submerging political contestation (Pierson 1993, pp. 609–610). These effects can differ substantially over time and across populations. In her study of Medicaid in the United States, for example, Michener (2018) reminds us of the importance of examining both the immediate impacts of the expansion of policies and the longer-term experiences citizens have as state officials enact those policies. These feedback effects also impact officials, whose expectations and behaviors change alongside those of everyday citizens.

To date, the literature on feedback effects has largely focused on how the experience of the welfare state shapes civic engagement in advanced industrialized countries (e.g., Campbell 2012; Mettler and Soss 2004; Soss and Schram 2007; Michener 2018; Hacker and Pierson 2019). Our study is one of a small but growing number that seeks to adapt a policy feedback framework to less developed contexts (Kruks-Wisner 2018a; Kumar 2022; MacLean 2011), to explore feedback effects in settings marked both by rule bending on the part of officials and by uneven state capacity. Our focus is thus on the implementation and institutionalization of policies, rather than on their formation, examining how bureaucratic actions (or inaction) can draw citizens into or away from the state.

As described in Section 2, the expansion of de jure rights sets the stage for claim-making. But we know that claim-making does not stop with a singular or momentary increase in demands on the state. Here, we explore what comes next, after citizens have stood in line, knocked on doors, attended hearings and meetings, and implored state officials to make good on their promises. We theorize a typology of feedback effects, reflecting what we term "positive," "negative," and "ambivalent" dynamics. The state shapes the initial terrain for claim-making through legislation and policymaking, and through the (variable) development of administrative and judicial apparatuses for implementation and fulfillment. Figure 5 depicts the recursive ways in which citizens might engage this terrain, and in which the state might respond (or not) to those claims. We describe state action on a continuum from unresponsive to fully responsive (top to bottom of the rectangle). Between these two poles is the intermediate condition of "partial" responsiveness.[44] In the case of partial responsiveness, state officials may engage with the claimant, but may not be able or willing to fully resolve the issue in a way that the claimant views as sufficient.[45]

---

[44] These dynamics do not necessarily represent stable equilibria, and even when a context is primarily defined by one type of feedback, individual experiences remain heterogeneous.

[45] Claim-making might be met with partial responsiveness for a wide range of reasons. Here, we are most concerned with how citizens *interpret* state responsiveness, and how this shapes their future claim-making.

Following state response (or lack thereof), claimants (as well as potential new claimants who have learned by watching) must decide whether to opt out of claim-making or to engage once again. Figure 5 illustrates how a fully unresponsive state funnels fewer claimants back into the feedback loop, while a state that always responds to citizens' claims, holding all else equal, provides the clearest incentives for claimants to continue to engage in claim-making. A partially responsive state lies in the middle: officials respond some of the time, leaving citizens to assess whether their continued efforts are worth the costs or whether they should give up or opt out. In opting out from claim-making, citizens may engage in different forms of exit, ranging from doing nothing, to seeking out private (market) alternatives, to rebellion (joining rebels or gangs). They might also continue to engage the state, but through agenda-setting politics in an effort to reshape policy (rather than allocative) responsiveness. Importantly, these different routes are not mutually exclusive: claimants can persist in the face of a non-responsive state; and opt out even when met with responsiveness. They can also engage in multiple strategies both at once and sequentially, for example pursuing a tutela claim while also joining a social movement that advocates changing laws around access to healthcare.

These patterns of iterative state engagement (or nonengagement) can be stylized as three unique types of feedback dynamics, defined by positive, negative, and ambivalent returns. To be clear, "positive" and "negative" returns are assessed not in terms of normative outcomes (good or bad), but in terms of whether a cycle of claim-making is (positively) continued or (negatively) disrupted. Positive feedback involves "a self-reinforcing process that

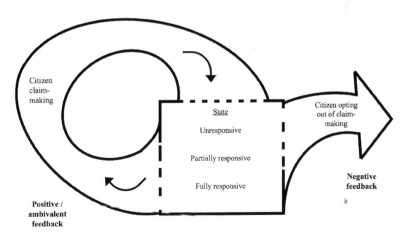

Figure 5 Feedback effects: claim-making and state response.

accentuates rather than counterbalances a trend" (Baumgartner and Jones 2002, p. 15). Each part of the process feeds into the other parts, making continuity more and more likely. In other words, positive feedback refers to the continuation of the claim-making process, but not necessarily the nature of the outcome. Negative feedback, on the other hand, discourages continuity. The process becomes self-undermining, leading to diminished or disrupted claim-making.

We theorize, in addition, a third kind of dynamic, which we call ambivalent feedback. Ambivalent feedback can lead to continued claim-making without the realization – or even expectation – of purely positive returns. In the short term, positive and ambivalent feedback are observationally equivalent: claim-making continues. Their differences become clear, however, with a longer time horizon. Positive returns continually propel claim-making forward in a self-sustaining loop. In the absence of these long-term positive returns, ambivalent feedback dynamics are more unstable, and can erode into negative dynamics. At times, however, ambivalent effects persist largely because claim-making practices have been institutionalized in ways that may not be directly tied to the observable outcomes of claims.[46]

Positive Feedback

A positive feedback effect occurs when claim-making is met with at least a degree of state responsiveness, and when that responsiveness begets future claim-making. Eventually, claim-making may come to form a central part of the way things are done. It becomes, in other words, a normalized and even institutionalized practice, becoming viewed by citizens as necessary and simply part of how the government works. We can write out the process of positive feedback as follows:

Claim-making → (Sufficient) Responsiveness → Citizen buy-in → Continued claim-making

Here, citizen claim-making and state responsiveness can create a positive loop, with claim-making reinforcing responsiveness to those claims and responsiveness incentivizing further claim-making.

Evidence of feedback defined by such positive returns is rare, though not non-existent, across our country-issue cases – particularly when we look at the individual level. In the Colombian case, for example, one claimant explained that their family had filed a tutela claim in the past, and that they found it

---

[46] See Stern (2013) for a discussion of how ambivalence and ambiguity impact Chinese environmental litigation.

a relatively quick process. They concluded that the tutela "had worked well," noting that, in fact, "it is the only thing that functions – we use it because it works."[47] In India, similarly, citizens' claims for payment on government worksites, often in the form of citizen-led review of the payment records, have met with sufficient success that such "social audits" have become institutionalized practice across India, and are now a regular and expected feature of the National Rural Employment Guarantee program (Jenkins and Manor 2017; Veeraraghavan 2022). However, most claimants in and across our cases do not operate in a world of purely positive feedback.

Negative Feedback

A continued lack of responsiveness by the state can prompt negative feedback dynamics that lead citizens to opt out from future claim-making. Nonresponsiveness may stem from officials' intentional efforts to disregard citizens' claims, or from an inability to engage those claims due to resource or other constraints. What's key in either scenario is how citizens react to the state's inability or unwillingness. While citizens react heterogeneously – some may continue to engage in claim-making despite unresponsiveness – negative feedback dynamics work, on aggregate, to dampen citizen–state engagement. As citizens' hopes and expectations are raised but not realized they may become aggrieved by what they see as broken promises. This sense of grievance might drive them to confront the state, and so to engage in more claim-making; or, quite the opposite, could have a chilling effect (Kruks-Wisner 2018a, 2021). Alternatively, citizens may simply give up and cease seeking redress altogether. Evans (2020, p. 660) refers to this as a "despondency trap," noting that "if people seldom see ... change, they may become stuck in a despondency trap, moderate their ambitions, and reluctantly perpetuate the status quo." Written out, a negative feedback dynamic takes this stylized form:

Claim-making → Un-responsiveness → Despondency → Citizens opt out of claim-making

Negative feedback is perhaps clearest in the case of disappearances in Mexico. Faced with what many view as impenetrable bureaucracy in a state widely perceived as both incapable and uncaring, the vast majority of the families of the more than 100,000 people who have been disappeared do not engage in sustained claim-making. While many initially contact the police or other authorities, a combination of state ineffectiveness, fear, and emotional and financial costs, as well as not knowing how and where to make claims, deter

---

[47] Taylor interview, Bogotá, March 2017, 44.

most family members from reporting the disappearance, much less pursuing their rights to truth and justice.

Similar dynamics are visible in India, where a full quarter of those surveyed in Rajasthan reported having never engaged in any claim-making activity at all – reflecting deep-seated beliefs about the inaccessibility of the state. Still others, though, *do* engage in claim-making at first, but become quickly disillusioned when they do not see a direct impact. In these cases, the decision to opt out of claim-making is driven by an expectations gap, where initial beliefs in the promises of the state are dashed against ground realities. Elsewhere in India, for example, complainants at government grievance redressal hearings were found to be initially optimistic directly after their hearings, but deeply despondent just weeks later as a result of perceived inaction on their cases (Kruks-Wisner 2021).

Negative feedback is also visible in both the Colombian and South African cases. In Colombia, for example, one interviewee explained, "[The idea of the tutela is] to assert our rights, but that does not work … that is a lie, it does nothing for you."[48] Similarly, another noted that filing a tutela "seems to me a waste of time and above all fills the courts … the perception I have is that it is of no use."[49] While this perception was not the modal one among those interviewed, several respondents shared similar views. In those cases, the experience of filing unsuccessful tutela claims was enough to drive citizens out of the claim-making cycle.

In South Africa, members of Abahlali baseMjondolo, a housing rights collective organizing to resist evictions, explained that, despite legal protections and their own claim-making, their shacks were repeatedly razed by the Anti-Land Invasion Unit. City officials had come around to mark shacks corresponding to a court order disallowing eviction. But even with those markings, residents relayed their fear of leaving the shacks, as the Anti-Land Invasion Unit would still come to destroy them frequently, often burning everything inside. While some residents continued to fight back, some chose not to rebuild, fearing that their shacks and everything in them would just be destroyed again.[50] In deciding not to rebuild, they further disengaged from the legal system, coming to believe that legal claims would not offer them much of anything.

Ceasing to engage in claim-making can also entail engaging the state in other ways (such as turning to electoral or movement-based politics), or can involve forms of "exit" from the state, for example by seeking private alternatives. In the Mexican case, since the state so often refuses to search for the remains of the disappeared, citizens may decide to do this themselves. In one popular

---

[48] Taylor interview, Bogotá, March 2017, 29.   [49] Taylor interview, Bogotá, March 2017, 18.
[50] Taylor Fieldnotes November 20, 2018.

initiative, more than forty victim's organizations have joined National Search Brigades, where hundreds of people travel to sites of suspected unmarked graves and search for the remains of their missing loved ones. This self-provision has clear downsides: forensic work done by citizens can contaminate evidence, place them at risk, and create more confusion in a chaotic policy and legal environment. In rural India, citizens can also choose to self-provide, turning, for example, to private sources of healthcare or education, or digging their own wells for water. At an extreme, some might not simply exit the state, but reject it outright. As Ray (2003, p. 6) has warned, "the very process that raises aspirations must also fulfill those aspirations in the not-too-distant future, otherwise enhanced voice can all too easily turn to violent exit." While not common in the state of Rajasthan, these dynamics are seen elsewhere in rural India, where anywhere from three to six percent of districts are affected by Maoist-inspired Naxalite insurgencies. As this illustrates, the political stakes of claim-making are potentially high: when unanswered, claims being made on the state can turn into claims *against* it.

Ambivalent Feedback

What we observed in our country-issue cases, however, often could not be classified as neatly "positive" or "negative" feedback. Instead, the most prevalent form of feedback across our cases is best characterized as ambivalent. Ambivalent feedback dynamics unfold when citizens continue to engage in claim-making despite partial or non-responsiveness on the part of the state. We see, in other words, the endurance of a claim-making process even in the absence of continuously positive returns.

Claim-making → Partial or non-responsiveness → Ambivalence → Continued but fragile claim-making

We see ample evidence of ambivalent feedback in all of our cases. For example, despite using the tutela to file more and more claims each year, Colombians express uncertainty and even skepticism about both the process of filing claims and the likely outcome. Most, though, continue to file. As Taylor (2018, p. 362) has explained, citizens have come to view the tutela "as their only possible option for accessing something they want, whether that thing is the response to a petition request or access to a specific medication or formal recognition by the state." In other words, they do not necessarily expect to be met with responsiveness. A resident of Cali shared:

I have a relative who is very sick. I had to file tutela actions that said the health clinic would not do the surgery or give the medication. Sometimes they comply, and they attend to the patient. Many times, no ... [In these situations], you have to get an order of contempt or file another tutela or go to the media. The [first] tutela is not enough.[51]

Another resident of Bogotá questioned the legitimacy of the tutela process while also underscoring its necessity:

The only way to claim that right [to health] so that they listen is through the tutela. To me, sadly, we are forced to resort to this because health should be something that is automatically covered, but since it's not, we have to turn [to the tutela], and not everyone gets a satisfactory response.[52]

In these examples, we see that Colombians have accepted that the tutela is central to their ability to make claims. This claim-making endures even in the face of noncompliance and unsatisfactory orders.

In rural Rajasthan, residents expressed a similar ambivalence about their continued claim-making. As noted, most saw their efforts as effective – but only partially so. Few reported that their problems were solved outright, and most described claim-making as an ongoing undertaking that one must engage if there is any hope of accessing resources. In the words of one man: "Programs are there, schemes are there. But if you sit quietly with your arms crossed, who will possibly hear you? Only those people who go forward and are active capture the ear of officials."[53]

We also see ambivalent dynamics in the case of housing rights in South Africa. The shack-dwellers' collective Abahlali baseMjondolo won a high-profile case in which they challenged the legality of the KwaZulu-Natal government's "Slums Act." The South African Constitutional Court decided in favor of Abahlali, holding that the Act was unconstitutional as it would result in widespread evictions without the provision of alternative accommodation. Yet those involved with Abahlali to this day do not believe that legal victories will ensure their rights. They have experienced the limits of legal decisions first hand; despite having gained favorable court decisions, the local government routinely issued blanket orders meant to undermine the courts and allow evictions. Even so, Abahlali continues to turn to the courts to make legal claims, despite being unsure that it will work.

Mexican claimants seeking justice for their disappeared loved ones are also deeply ambivalent. Victims' collectives throughout the country have achieved an unwritten, though vitally important, advance in shrinking the gap between

---

[51] Taylor interview, Cali, April 15, 2017.　[52] Taylor interview, Bogotá, March 2017, 46.
[53] Kruks-Wisner interview, Udaipur district, December 15, 2010.

promised rights and their fulfillment. Ten years ago, when disappearances emerged as a phenomenon, victims commonly reported that state investigators would simply refuse to take the report of the disappearance, to sit down with family members to talk about the case, or to show them the case file. Through repeated and persistent claim-making, along with pressure exerted from both movements and activists, victims' collectives have slowly established the modality of participatory investigations. Yet victims commonly report being caught in a repetitive cycle of continuing meetings with minimal advances. The case of Amores, a victims collective in Monterrey, Mexico, is illustrative. Their monthly meetings with the Attorney General's office, over time, became, as one member recounted, "like a ritual":

> We went and sat and talked with the investigators, the police. And they would ask us what else we should do [in terms of the investigation] . . . and for a while we suggested things, and sometimes they did them. And we would complain and sometimes get angry . . . but they never did more [than we asked them to do]; they didn't have their own lines of investigation. But we keep going [to these meetings]—what else would we do? Go back to how we were?[54]

Ambivalent feedback is particularly likely to develop where the rights terrain is uneven. First, ambivalent effects are likely if citizens can see (or hear about) the state responding in different ways for others, provoking a sense of comparative grievance. These dynamics are also common in multi-level governance environments where one state actor might take responsive action but others do not; a higher-level official, for example, might give a directive that is not carried out at a lower-level, or lower-level actors might attempt resolution but lack the support or approval of higher officials. In a complex claim involving multiple agencies and steps, ambivalent feedback is especially likely to occur; progress can be stalled or stuck even after several successful steps. Citizens, in these cases, have seen some movement, but still find their rights unfulfilled. They are thus dissatisfied with the responses they receive, but may continue in the claim-making process in the hopes that they will see further action. That hope, though, can be fragile; the tipping point between an ambivalent and negative feedback loop is slippery.

Second, citizens may be compelled to continue claim-making if they feel that there is, quite simply, no alternative. In such cases, they may continue to make claims without necessarily buying into the value or effectiveness of claim-making – often with good reason to remain skeptical. They continue to engage in claim-making because the practice has become socially and institutionally

---

[54] Gallagher interview, Monterrey, March 23, 2012.

embedded; both citizens and officials come to see it as a normal, routine, and necessary part of how law is enforced and programs are implemented. This is again likely in complex claims, as people, having already undertaken several steps, fear sunk costs and sliding back to the beginning of the claim-making cycle if they stop pushing forward.

Third, and closely related, ambivalent feedback dynamics can also occur if the critical nature of the issue at hand simply compels claimants to continue. That is, no matter how unresponsive the state is, people continue claim-making because the stakes are so high. As Simmons (2014, 2016) argues, certain types of claims are especially salient in different cultural contexts; for example, access to water in Bolivia. Under these conditions, claim-making may feel like a Sisyphean task, but opting out is simply not an option.

Ambivalent feedback dynamics, however, are subject to instability over the long term. Without the momentum of positive returns, a sense of comparative grievance, the perceived lack of alternative, and/or the significance of the need must be strong enough to overcome the costs of claim-making as well as citizens' doubts about the utility of the endeavor. If these costs and doubts compile over time, the result may be that claimants are driven to exit. In other words, ambivalent feedback may erode into negative feedback.

Whether feedback effects are positive, negative, or ambivalent reflects the interplay between state capacity and citizens' expectations. A capacious state may be able to respond fully to every claim made by citizens (though its willingness to do so may be a different story). A state hampered in terms of capacity will be unable to do so. In assessing the effects of claim-making, we therefore need to take into account the ability of the state to respond, all else equal. Before turning to the Conclusion, we therefore examine several open questions about the relationship between claim-making and inequality, the implications of claim-making for democratic practice, and the impact of claim-making on the state itself.

Claim-Making and Inequality

The structural inequalities that shape citizens' access to the state suggest that claim-making may be more frequent as well as more necessary for those from less advantaged positions. In fiscally and capacity constrained states, where resources are distributed irregularly, the need for claim-making is likely to be higher among the poor than among the rich, who can turn more easily to private services or self-provisioning. This reflects a "two-tiered" system in which "those who [can] pay frequently [choose] to opt out of what the state [has] to offer" (MacLean 2011, p. 1155). This leaves the state "central to the lives of the poor even as it is diminished in the lives of the more well-to-do" (Kruks-Wisner

2018a, p. 34). Less privileged citizens, moreover, will encounter larger and more frequent gaps in the fulfillment of their rights – increasing the imperative for claim-making. These, however, are the same citizens to whom the state is often the least responsive, creating a paradox: those who most need to make claims on the state may also be the least likely to be successful in their efforts.

Similar tensions emerge with regard to informality. Claim-making rests in large part on the legal and policy commitments of the state. Yet claim-making is also practiced by those who may not enjoy the formal protection of the law, or for whom certain rights are not formally recognized. Residents of informal settlements, for example, regularly petition the state for rights (e.g., to housing or services) even given (and often because of) their "illegal" status as squatters. They do so, however, on the basis that the state has, at least for some people in some settings, articulated those rights. Brazil's 1988 Constitution, for example, famously affirmed social rights to housing, health, and education, which squatter communities subsequently began to claim to justify "land invasions" and to further demand services in their "insurgent" communities (Holston 2008). The same is true for India in the case of urban informal settlements, where residents actively pursue resources and protections at the same time that they contend with the predation of the state in the form of evictions (Auerbach 2019). Similar dynamics are observed in South Africa, where those living in informal settlements have organized to oppose eviction attempts. In these cases, residents of informal settlements are engaged in claim-making in an effort to *extend* existing rights commitments. Here, too, there is a paradox: those who are least protected by law may have the greatest need to make legal claims on the state.

These paradoxes reflect underlying inequalities in social class, economic standing, and legal status that differentiate everyday experiences of citizenship (Holston 2008). Claim-making can both mitigate and reinforce these forms of inequality. In cases where the poor and marginalized are successful claim-makers, their efforts may help to reduce inequality by bringing their levels of rights fulfillment closer to those of the more wealthy or powerful. The possibility of collective claims, in particular, can disrupt entrenched patterns of exclusion. In South Africa, for example, housing rights petitions have had most success when part of settlement-wide claims against evictions, benefiting large swaths of population within a city. Individual claims can also bring about wider collective gains, with broad distributional consequences. Successful claims to the right to work through the National Rural Employment Guarantee in India, for example, have not only resulted in unprecedented financial gains to individual beneficiaries (raising household earnings by as much as 14 percent, by one estimate); it has also altered rural labor markets, driving an increase in private-sector wages and an overall reduction in poverty rates (Muralidharan et al. 2023). Even when brought forward by more privileged citizens, some claims can also bring about wider gains. For instance, middle- and upper-class citizens have, as individuals, benefited disproportionately from filing tutela claims in Colombia. However, as Uprimny Yepes and Durán (2014, p. 6 emphasis added) note, "the judicial protection of health has also had *aggregate* effects because it has triggered other processes of a more structural nature, and these general impacts often end up benefiting the most excluded and poor sectors of society." In other words, individual claims can sometimes have radiating effects, provoking changes that benefit everyone (Rodríguez Garavito 2011).

But claim-making can also drive inequality. To make claims requires citizens to expend resources and time; claimants must wait in line or attend meeting after meeting. They must pay for transit, printing and copying services, and childcare, among other things. It follows that those with the fewest resources to spare will find claim-making the most costly, even as they are likely to need to engage in it the most. Claim-making can also widen gaps *among* the poor and marginalized, if those who make successful claims move toward becoming rights-bearing and resource-receiving "haves," while those who either do not make claims or are less successful in doing so remain "have nots" (Galanter 1974).

Claim-making can also reinforce existing power differentials. When citizens stand on unequal footing, claim-making can deepen distinctions between those for whom it is a last or only resort and those who already enjoy more privileged access to the state. In affluent communities, for example, claim-making can take on aspects of exclusionary "NIMBYism," if residents demand action to protect their privileged standing. For example, as Einstein et al. (2019, p. 4) write of US cities, "those who participate in local housing politics ... use their privileged status as members of a community to prevent new housing, and thus close its doors to new members." In South Africa, similarly, Anti-Land Invasion Units, used to respond to "illegal occupancy or land invasions," are often called upon by those from relatively more affluent backgrounds. Claim-making of this kind, when driven by those from more elite backgrounds, can serve to protect narrow class interests.

The a priori effects of claim-making on inequality are thus ambiguous. While a critical pathway to resources for individual claimants, it is not necessarily a grand equalizer on aggregate. The articulation and negotiation of claims at the local level, particularly in deeply divided settings, can reinforce and engender existing and new inequalities. In a world where citizens are stratified by class, caste, race, gender, and other cleavages – and where some enjoy greater and more preferential access to brokers, political representatives, and other linkages to the state – citizens' capacity for claim-making, and the state's responsiveness to their claims, can never be equal.

Claim-Making and Citizenship Practice

Another set of questions emerges about how we should interpret acts of claim-making within the study of democratic participation. Claimants who approach officials without (or at least not fully reliant on) political intermediation do so, at least in part, on the basis of their standing as "rights-bearing citizens." Direct claim-making, in this sense, has much in common with what Houtzager and Acharya (2011, p. 6) have referred to as "institutionalized petitioning," where "citizens make direct claims on public bureaucracy through channels that are known, formal, and universally accessible," and which they operationalized in terms of "seeking out government officials in person," and "bringing a legal case to force some kind of government action" (p.12). This form of citizen practice, Houtzager and Acharya (2011, p. 6) write, "most closely approximates the democratic ideal" in that the channels engaged "guarantee universal access and equal treatment under the law."

We, however, depart from the assumption that channels of access to public agencies are universally accessible, or that the treatment citizens receive in those spaces are rule-bound or equal. Far from it, we see the variability of citizens' access and treatment as a key driver of claim-making, which, as demonstrated in Section 2, unfolds on the basis of rights guarantees even as (and *because*) those rights are not regularly realized. We also do not place a prescribed normative value on direct practices simply because they are direct. Formal institutions and direct practices are – just like the informal and indirect – power-laden and easily captured, leaving it unclear that they are any more equitable than mediated approaches or brokered spaces.

At issue then, is what Bertorelli et al. (2017) refer to as the "quality" of citizenship practice entailed in claim-making. "Effective" citizenship, they suggest, can be understood as the ability to engage the state as "bearer of rights, and not as supplicant, client, or subject" (Bertorelli et al. 2017, p. 9). Claim-making, as a form of citizenship practice, is not always "effective" in this sense; it is enabled by written rights, but required precisely because those rights are not adequately realized. Seen in this light, claim-making might be interpreted as a series of desperate, stop-gap measures by citizens who, far from being "rights bearing," instead negotiate "unstable and sub-optimal arrangements for service delivery" (Heller et al. 2015, p. 32). But claimants are also not simply clients or subjects. They approach the state with rights in hand (and on paper), in spaces that are neither rule-bound nor rule free. Whether and how these practices become a pathway to "effective" citizenship, where people are able to enjoy their rights without constantly having to claim them, are open and pressing questions. The answers, we suggest, hinge largely on the capacity and willingness of the state to respond, and how citizens perceive and react to state responses.

The high levels of claim-making that we have documented across our cases are indicative of a striking level of engagement with the state, even and expressly among some of the most marginalized. That these practices unfold not simply through clientelist and partisan networks suggests, moreover, citizenries that – far from being narrowly dependent on patron–client relationships – navigate access to the state in a diversity of ways. One interpretation of these dynamics is that they might represent the beginnings of a shift away from non-programmatic and clientelist politics, driven by structural changes in both governance institutions and in citizenship practices that "erode the efficiency of [partisan] brokers" (Stokes et al. 2013, p. 21). A different interpretation, however, might focus on the necessity of claim-making in settings that remain decidedly non-programmatic; the yawning gap between the promises and actions of the state, and between written rules and their application, are what make claim-making not only common but also essential. This, in turn, might suggest a democratic deficit, as citizens are forced to make claims for resources and protections that ought to already be theirs. High rates of claim-making in and among marginalized communities might, in this view, be seen as indicative of the inaccessibility of the state, as well as of patterns of exclusion that compel marginalized citizens to do the work of attempting to convert rights into lived realities.

As we have suggested, the reality likely lies somewhere in between. Claim-making unfolds within, and so may serve to broaden, the spaces between programmatic and non-programmatic politics; it reveals the salience and fragility of rules, which enable and provoke claim-making by being both written (publicly observable in law and policy) and broken (creating the gaps that necessitate citizen action). As the institutional terrain of the state shifts, and as more and more citizens directly engage unelected state officials to make demands, claim-making practice may become a recognizable, expected, and in turn more deeply institutionalized set of practices.

Claim-Making and State Responsiveness

A related set of questions concerns whether and how claim-making might, over time, qualitatively shift patterns of state responsiveness. In considering impacts on the state, we build on Mann's concept of state infrastructural power: "the institutional capacity of a central state ... to penetrate its territories and logistically implement decisions" (Mann 1984, p. 113). Infrastructural power, in contrast to states' "despotic" power to enact decisions without social consent, refers to the ability to govern *through* civil society to implement policy and realize social projects. But, as Soifer and vom Hau (2008) caution, those projects can encompass forms of social control as well as the delivery of public goods. Infrastructural power can thus be expressed in different ways, in different arenas of citizen–state engagement. Claim-making occurs in these arenas and can, as Soifer and vom Hau predicted, both bolster and undermine the state.

Turning first to healthcare in Colombia, the growth and persistence of tutela claims suggest that claim-making can create a toehold for citizens, prompting the state toward greater responsiveness. Claim-making related to the healthcare system has prompted judges to reinterpret and expand the meaning of right to health (Taylor 2020a). What's more, as citizens have continued to make tutela claims over the last thirty years, the relative power of the main actor overseeing the tutela – the Constitutional Court – has increased. Many citizens report generally positive views of the tutela and the Constitutional Court, while disparaging the rest of the legal system (Taylor 2018). And as Landau (2010, p. 153) demonstrates, the Constitutional Court has managed to weather a variety of efforts by the executive and legislative branches to limit its power by framing itself as the "workhorse for middle-class claims." Claim-making through the tutela has shored up the power of the Constitutional Court, which in turn has created greater space for further claim-making. The result is not a system without flaws, but citizens gain at least the opportunity to pursue their interests in one additional forum, and the Constitutional Court gains prominence and protection within and from the rest of the state.

As in Colombia, the case of housing rights in South Africa shows how claim-making can lead to significant, if also narrow, developments in the struggle for rights realizations. As one South African lawyer summarized, in early housing rights cases, judges "invariably referred to our clients as 'building hijackers,' 'criminals,' 'the lowest of the low.'"[55] Over time, the narrative and the way that judges see these claimants has changed. Now, they may be "unlawful occupiers," but the understanding is they are handcuffed by poverty. These semantic shifts (not insignificant in themselves) were accompanied by changes in jurisprudence that offer substantial regulations to govern the process of evictions. Now claim-making around evictions almost follows "a handbook," as that same lawyer described.[56] Illegal evictions still occur, and many remain without access to adequate housing. Yet legal claim-making provides an avenue through which citizens can push the state to respond to their needs, at the very least offering a fair process and a way to avoid homelessness.

---

[55] Taylor interview, Johannesburg, August 28, 2018.
[56] Taylor interview, Johannesburg, August 28, 2018.

In India, too, continued claim-making has helped to not only realize but also institutionalize rights in ways that have provoked ground shifts in both citizens' and officials' legal consciousness. As more expansive social policy was written into law, citizens' expectations of the state grew; there is, simply put, "more state" in the form of social protection policies and programs, leading to greater citizen–state encounters. These encounters, in turn, have reshaped the work of local governments, which are called on to administer a growing array of programs, and of local administrators who have taken on an enlarged set of tasks including social audits, grievance redressal, and other processes explicitly designed to respond to citizens' claims (Adhikari and Heller 2022; Veeraraghavan 2022).

The right to work established by the National Rural Employment Guarantee offers a prime example. While written into law in 2005, the right to work only became effectively realized as groups of citizens made claims in informal public hearings, demanding access to documents and reading out loud the names of program beneficiaries and the amounts paid. Over time, the state itself has taken up the practice, encouraging both governmental and civil society actors to conduct social audits (Jenkins and Manor 2017; Veeraraghavan 2022). There are many gaps in the audit system, and the employment guarantee program remains infamously uneven in its administration. And yet, over time, the right to work has become more deeply embedded: socially (in public imaginations and expectations of the state), economically (in real wages paid), and within the bureaucracy (in new practices developed to implement and monitor the program). In this instance, citizen claim-making helped to actualize a new right. The (partial) realization of that right, in turn, activated citizens, who through their demands, pushed the state to create new institutions to further implement the right.

Similar to India, perhaps the most remarkable change in Mexico has been a shift in the national consciousness regarding what it means to be disappeared. Prior to the sustained claim-making of the family members of the disappeared, state discourse and public opinion had successfully hidden the problem, blamed the victims, and ensured blanket impunity in cases of disappearances. Sustained claim-making carved out space within a broad range of state institutions to listen to the voices of the families of the disappeared. Gone is state discourse blaming the victims, and leaders of victims' collective are now invited to meet with politicians, give talks in Mexican universities, and regularly profiled in the media. Victims' families have also compelled officials to engage in participatory *mesas de trabajo*, forcing a dramatic shift in the behavior and accessibility of the police, state investigators, and other judicial actors. While the gains from these participatory investigations remain limited, they mark a transformation in citizen–state engagement in a context that was previously impenetrable for and explicitly hostile to most citizens. This represents a norm shift around access to justice; while it is still rare for a perpetrator to be convicted for the crime of a disappearance, it is now fairly common for victims to have access to their case files, to meet with the state officials tasked with investigating their case, and for basic investigatory steps to be taken.

As claimants have pushed for justice, the Mexican state has passed new legislation and created a plethora of new institutions. In 2012, the National Human Rights Commission formed an agency with the mission of supporting victims in their search for their loved ones, which was then expanded upon in 2013 in victims' rights legislation. Part of the mission (and budget) of these newly created agencies and legislation has been to provide victims with financial support for the costs associated with searching for their loved one, including traveling to different parts of the country for meetings with investigatory officials. In 2017, national legislation written by a coalition of victims' collectives finally criminalized enforced disappearances in all of Mexico's thirty-two states, and also mandated a national database of the disappeared and of the DNA of their family members. It also requires a more rigorous investigatory protocol. While no one is surprised that this law has not been fully implemented, it has expanded the legal rights available for victims to claim.

In all of these instances, citizen claim-making has worked to provoke shifts in governance practices as well as in the administrative and judicial institutions – for example, the tutela, the social audit, the *mesas de trabajo* – where these practices unfold. Together, these examples suggest the possibility that claim-making can shift the terrain upon which claims are made. Yet it is far from clear that claim-making, on aggregate, will push a transformation toward a more inclusive state. The very existence of claim-making as mode of distributive politics allows for some discretion or selectivity on the part of officials in the allocation of resources and the expenditure of their efforts. The onus therefore remains on citizens to extract resources from the state. This is, in some ways, a suboptimal arrangement; but it is nonetheless an arrangement that, for many people in many places, is widening access to the state.

Conclusions and Further Directions

We began with the stories of citizens scrambling to gain access to truth and justice, to healthcare, to stays of evictions, to employment, and to drinking water. These citizens did not simply turn to elected officials, or to established social movements. Nor did they give up on the possibility of state provision or on the fulfillment of their rights. Instead, they sought to press public personnel in administrative and judicial institutions. In so doing, they entered spaces beyond the ballot and the barricade to make claims on the state. Some of the time, it worked. Other times, their efforts were frustrated and their claims left unheard.

Claim-making of this kind has become a pervasive form of citizenship practice, with important material and distributional consequences, yet it has remained largely outside the gaze of political science. In this Element, we have offered a framework through which to theorize and explore everyday claim-making. In Section 1, we defined claim-making as citizen action in pursuit of rights and entitlements, which emerges in response to state practices that are neither fully rule-bound nor centered exclusively on partisan actors. Claim-making, we argued, unfolds in the spaces between programmatic and non-programmatic service delivery. It interacts with but is not bound by electoral politics, reflecting citizens' efforts – direct and mediated – to convince state officials to act on their behalf. This everyday and often localized nature also makes it distinct from the mass mobilization of social movements, which may create supportive conditions for claim-making, but which are largely absent from many citizens' quotidian repertoires of action.

In Section 2, we examined the conditions that make claim-making prevalent in settings marked by inequality and uneven state performance, through a combination of both "push" and "pull" factors. In our cases, as in much of the global south, the emergence of neoliberal policy orthodoxy created mounting pressure to reduce the size of the state and to limit social spending, while established vehicles for representing the interests of marginalized citizens, such as left-wing or worker parties and labor unions, withered. At the same time, formal state commitments to citizenship rights expanded dramatically, and with these new avenues for claim-making opened up. The results were states with by a robust set of de jure rights but with inconsistent de facto ability or willingness to realize those commitments. These conditions – marked by the unevenness of the state's rights terrain – created both the possibility and need to make claims. Citizens became increasingly aware of the promises of the state, and of the gaps where those promises were unmet. Appointed state officials, moreover, became increasingly accessible, in large part due to a proliferation of institutions designed to facilitate claim-making: legal procedures, grievance platforms, participatory institutions, and other access mechanisms.

In Section 3, we explored the consequences of claim-making, demonstrating that this citizen action does, some of the time, impact the provision of public goods, services, and protections. The material consequences for individual claimants can be dramatic: access to a life-saving medication, the stay of an eviction order, a more reliable source of drinking water, or the uncovering of new information about what happened to a missing loved one. But claim-making does not work for everyone in every circumstance. Nor is it an easy or universal undertaking. The distributional consequences of this unevenness, both in who makes claims and in the responsiveness of officials, are far reaching. Where claim-making is taken on by those with the least access to resources, it can potentially lead to more inclusive distribution of goods, services, and protections. But when claim-making is concentrated among more privileged groups of citizens, it can be regressive – expanding access to resources for some while leaving those with the least farther behind. Claim-making thus has the potential to drive or mitigate inequality.

The experience of making claims alters citizens' expectations of the state. Section 3 therefore also explored the effects on continued and future citizenship practice. The returns to claim-making are "positive" (and so self-perpetuating) if and when it serves, in real and material terms, to broaden citizens' access in ways that inspire further citizen action. "Negative" feedback occurs when citizens, despite active claim-making, see little if any response and so, over time, turn away from the state. These fully positive and negative scenarios, however, diverge from much of what we observed in practice. Instead, we noted the frequency of ambivalent dynamics, where claim-making is met with mixed, partial, and at times performative responses from the state, resulting in marginal and inconsistent improvements in citizens' access to goods or services. The continuance of claim-making in such cases is fragile, and can easily tip toward negative dynamics. Other times, however, ambivalent feedback persists, taking on a logic and a stasis of its own: citizens make claims on the state because they have to, without necessarily seeing systemic shifts in state responsiveness.

The Claim-Making Agenda: Questions for Future Research

Our country-issue cases, as noted in the Introduction, were not selected with comparison in mind. While this restricted our ability to engage in controlled comparisons, it opened up rich avenues for *contextualized* comparison, enabling us to examine common and varied claim-making practices, conditions, and consequences across different sectors, rights arenas, and institutional settings.

Our hope is that our exploration of claim-making within and across these different cases provides a springboard for more systematic, comparative, and longitudinal study. We therefore conclude by considering several sets of questions, extending from and beyond the cases we have explored here, about different types of claim-making strategy, the material and political consequences of claim-making, and variation in claim-making across space and over time.

Varieties of Claim-Making

As our cases demonstrate, claim-making can unfold through different channels, and be undertaken by different actors. Delineating this range of practices – and understanding when and why claimants pursue particular strategies – is of critical importance. When, for example, is claim-making likely to be direct, and when is it likely to be mediated through brokered channels? Future research should systematically probe the incentives facing social and political brokers, their impact on the claim-making process, and their relative prevalence in different contexts. Further research is also required to explore claim-making under different institutional conditions. The surrounding institutional environment, and in particular the density of party networks and/or the presence of associations or other collective bodies, clearly plays a role in shaping pathways to claim-making. This, however, provokes the question of whether and how claim-making might empower or constrain partisan actors and brokers. How, in particular, might claim-making reshape the allocative and distributive roles of parties? If claim-making occurs in the space between programmatic and non-programmatic politics, can it also work to enlarge that space?

Claim-making also varies in the actors and agencies targeted and in the strategies employed. Our research, for example, highlights claim-making in both bureaucratic and judicial arenas. More study is needed to explore whether and how claim-making differs across these arenas, as well as why citizens might opt to undertake legal strategies in some instances and turn to bureaucrats in others. Here too the underlying institutional environment plays a key role, making certain strategies more attractive or viable than others. Consider, for example, how the recognition of social rights in India as "directive principles" rather than constitutional rights incentivized a turn to bureaucratic rather than legal arenas. Similarly, the institutional design of the tutela enabled individualized legal claim-making in Colombia, while the nature of South African courts demanded collective legal claims – often of a more mediated nature. At the level of the individual, claimants can also deliberately move from one strategy to another. This prompts questions about when and why people pursue particular strategies. Why, for example, does someone in one moment file an individual petition with a local bureaucrat and in another initiate a formal legal claim as part of a collective? How do these different claim-making strategies build on or feed into one another?

Claim-Making Efficacy

A related line of inquiry stems from the question of when and why different claim-making strategies are more or less likely to "work." In Section 3, we tracked the consequences of claim-making in each of our country-issue cases. The record is decidedly mixed, raising critical questions about when claim-making is most effective. A first set of questions centers on the officials who are the targets of claim-making. If not fully motivated by partisan or electoral logics, how should we make sense of what drives state officials, bureaucrats, and functionaries? As Maynard-Moody and Musheno (2000, p. 329) note, there are two dominant perspectives on the motivation of appointed local officials. One emphasizes discretion and self-interest; specifically, the desire of bureaucrats to "make their work easier, safer, and more rewarding." The second suggests that bureaucrats instead "base their decisions on their judgment of the worth [and circumstances] of the individual citizens" rather than on overarching policy agendas or self-interest. Our research suggests that these perspectives can be woven together, as state officials respond (or not) along multiple dimensions. In Mexico, for example, Gallagher found in interviews with public prosecutors that some viewed themselves as crusaders who placed a higher value on public service than on their own safety, wealth, and professional advancement. Others, however, were more responsive to incentives for advancement, enrichment, and safety in the local context. There is pressing need for greater research on the factors that spark and sustain bureaucratic responsiveness to citizens' claims.

A second set of questions on claim-making efficacy takes the perspective of claimants, asking what counts as a "success"? How might the goals of different claimants vary? Some may be content to "name and shame," while others seek material resolution of a problem, and others still may act with the intent to spur fundamental social or political changes. How might claimants' goals impact both their choice of strategies and the impact of their efforts? How, moreover, do these varied goals affect long-term trends in claim-making and the feedback dynamics described in Section 3? The tipping points between these different effects – positive, negative, and ambivalent – and the factors that drive movement from one to another, are critical dynamics that will require longitudinal study. Can claim-making, over time, draw more citizens into the political arena and provoke greater responsiveness among officials? Or might claim-making – and the inequalities that underlie and provoke it – hinder the development of a more inclusive state dedicated to more uniform patterns of public provision and rights fulfillment?

Claim-Making across Space and Time

A third set of questions, moving farther afield from our study cases, focuses on variation in the likelihood, prevalence, and typologies of claim-making across different geographical and institutional settings, as well as at different historical moments. In Section 2, we theorize that claim-making is most likely under conditions of unevenness, given gaps between de jure commitments and de facto fulfillment of rights. Further research is needed to explore the factors that produce such unevenness, looking beyond the relatively recent moves toward neoliberalism on the one hand and social legislation on the other. The dynamics that push and pull citizens into claim-making may look different in different regions, under different political economic conditions, and at different moments in time. Future research might also explore whether and how different push and pull factors drive unevenness in other historical periods. How has claim-making, as a form of citizenship practice, changed over time?

In Section 2, we also theorized the conditions that would be less conducive to claim-making: those of scarcity (where there are limited rights commitments and few resources to claim) and of abundance (where there are expansive commitments that are readily and regularly realized). Under both of these sets of conditions, we posit that claim-making has less utility and so will be more limited. These are testable predictions, requiring systematic study of the prevalence of claim-making under different conditions – a task we could not take on with our country-issue cases. Broader comparative study of claim-making across different institutional and regional settings is required to probe these dynamics further. It could be that our predictions are too black and white; claim-making might still unfold under conditions of scarcity or abundance, but take different forms that we have yet to fully consider.

A similar blind spot in our current study cases is that all are at least procedurally democratic. Two are relatively young democracies (Mexico and South Africa), while two have long, if troubled, histories with democracy (Colombia and India). This does not mean, however, that claim-making does not occur in nondemocratic settings; far from it, scholarship focused on authoritarian contexts has detailed similarly diverse and intensive citizen-led claim-making.[57] Future research should more systematically explore the contours of claim-making in settings defined by different regime types. As the literature on authoritarianism reminds us, it is necessary to look more closely at the forms of citizenship practice that unfold in the absence of contested elections. Even with

---

[57] See for example work on East Germany (Lueders 2021), Egypt (El-Ghobashy 2021), Iraq (Walter 2018), the Soviet Union (Dimitrov 2014), Sudan (Massoud 2013), and China (e.g., O'Brien 1996; O'Brien and Li 2006; Gallagher 2006, 2017; Michelson 2007; Stern 2013).

elections, democratic contexts can be defined by illiberalism, especially for particular subsets of the population, and authoritarian contexts can be defined by degrees of liberalism (McCann and Kahraman 2021). How do these dynamics influence how claim-making plays out? How do opportunities for bureaucratic and legal claim-making function under different democratic and nondemocratic conditions?

***

The questions we have posed point to the importance of further research on claim-making. Developing this research agenda, in all its complexity, is a critical undertaking. To do so will require careful attention to quotidian practices by citizens, often overlooked in the shadow of more dramatic and well-studied events such as elections and mass mobilization. But if we follow the lead of citizens themselves, our attention is drawn to diverse forms of everyday engagement that take place between and beyond punctuated moments of voting or protesting, and which unfold in spaces that are neither fully clientelistic nor programmatic. These seemingly mundane acts of claim-making, we have argued, are increasingly common and consequential forms of citizenship practice. Close, careful, and comparative study of claim-making is required to develop a more nuanced and complete understanding of citizens' efforts to narrow the gap between the promises and actions of the state. To do so will cast important new light on political participation and distributive politics, as seen from the bottom up by ordinary citizens.

References

Adhikari, A. (2023). Redeeming Right and Democratization of the Local State in India. Doctoral dissertation, Brown University.

Adhikari, A. and Heller, P. (2022). "Civil Society, the State and Institutionalizing Welfare Rights in India." Unpublished manuscript.

African National Congress Constitutional Committee. (1990). *A Bill of Rights for a New South Africa: A Working Document*. Centre for Development Studies.

Alexander, J. and Fernandez, K. (2021). "The Impact of Neoliberalism on Civil Society and Nonprofit Advocacy." *Nonprofit Policy Forum* 12(2): 367–394.

Auerbach, A. M. (2019). *Demanding Development*. Cambridge University Press.

Auerbach, A. M. and Kruks-Wisner, G. (2020). "The Geography of Citizenship Practice: How the Poor Engage the State in Rural and Urban India." *Perspectives on Politics* 18(4): 1118–1134.

Auerbach, A. M. and Thachil, T. (2018). "How Clients Select Brokers: Competition and Choice in India's Slums." *American Political Science Review*, 112(4), 775–791.

(2023). *Migrants and Machine Politics*. Princeton University Press.

Baldwin K. (2016). *The Paradox of Traditional Leaders in Democratic Africa*. Cambridge University Press.

Baccaro, L. and Howell, C. (2017). *Trajectories of Neoliberal Transformation*. Cambridge University Press.

Banerjee, A. (2004). "Who Is Getting the Public Goods in India? Some Evidence and Some Speculation." In *India's Emerging* Economy. Edited by K. Basu. MIT Press, 183–214.

Baumgartner, F. R. and Jones, B. D. (2002). *Policy Dynamics*. University of Chicago Press.

BBC News. (2019). "South Africa Elections: Has the ANC Built Enough Homes?" May 3, 2019, sec. Africa.

Bertorelli, E., Heller, P., Swaminathan, S., and Varshney, A. (2017). "Does Citizenship Abate Class? Evidence and Reflections from a South Indian City." *Economic and Political Weekly* 52(32): 47–57.

Boughton, J. M. (2012). *Tearing Down Walls*. International Monetary Fund.

Boulding, C., and Holzner, C. (2020). "Community Organizations and Latin America's Poorest Citizens: Voting, Protesting, and Contacting Government." *Latin American Politics and Society* 62(4): 98–125.

(2021). *Voice and Inequality*. Oxford University Press.

Bøttkjær, L. and Justesen, M. K. (2021). "Why Do Voters Support Corrupt Politicians? Experimental Evidence from South Africa." *Journal of Politics* 83(2): 788–793.

Brinks, D. M. (2012). "The Transformation of the Latin American State-as-Law" *Revista de Ciencia Política* 32(3): 561–583.

Brinks, D. M., Gauri, V., and Shen, K. (2015). "Social Rights Constitutionalism: Negotiating the Tension Between the Universal and the Particular." *Annual Review of Law and Social Science* 11(1): 289–308.

Bussell, J. (2012). *Corruption and Reform in India.* Cambridge University Press.

(2019). *Clients and Constituents.* Oxford University Press.

Campbell, A. (2012). "Policy Makes Mass Politics." *Annual Review of Political Science* 15(1): 333–351.

Carlin, R. E., Castrellón, M., Gauri, V., Jaramillo Sierra, I. C., and Staton, J. K. (2022). "Public Reactions to Noncompliance with Judicial Orders." *American Political Science Review* 116 (1): 265–282.

Chandra, K. (2004). *Why Ethnic Parties Succeed.* Cambridge University Press.

Chipkin, I., Swilling, M., Bhorat, H, et al. (2018). *Shadow State: The Politics of State Capture.* Johannesburg: Wits University Press.

Collier, R. B., and Handlin, S. (2009). *Reorganizing Popular Politics.* Penn State Press.

Dasgupta, A. and Kapur, D. (2020). "The Political Economy of Bureaucratic Overload: Evidence from Rural Development Officials in India." *American Political Science Review* 114(4): 1316–1334.

de Kadt, D. and Larreguy, H. A. (2018). "Agents of the Regime? Traditional Leaders and Electoral Politics in South Africa." *Journal of Politics* 80(2): 382–399.

Del Mistro, R. and Hensher, D. A. (2009). "Upgrading Informal Settlements in South Africa: Policy, Rhetoric and What Residents Really Value." *Housing Studies* 24(3): 333–354.

Defensoría del Pueblo (2020). "La Tutela y los derecho a la salud y a la seguridad social, 2019." On file with the authors. www.defensoria.gov .co/web/guest/-/la-tutela-y-los-derechos-a-la-salud-y-a-la-seguridad-social-14%C2%B0-edici%C3%B3n?p_l_back_url=%2Fweb%2Fguest %2Fsearch%3Fq%3Dla%2Btutela%2By%2Blos%2Bderechos%2Ba %2Bla%2Bsalud%2B2019

Dimitrov, M. (2014). "Tracking Public Opinion under Authoritarianism." *Russian History* 41(3): 329–353.

Ding, I. (2020). "Performative Governance." *World Politics* 72(4): 525–556.

Drèze, J. and Sen, A. (2013). An Uncertain Glory: India and Its Contradictions. Princeton University Press.

Dugard, J. (2015). "Closing the Doors of Justice: An Examination of the Constitutional Court's Approach to Direct Access." *South African Journal on Human Rights* 31(1): 112–135.

Dunning, T. (2009). "Direct Action and Associational Participation: Problem-Solving Repertoires of Individuals." In *Reorganizing Popular Politics*. Edited by R. B. Collier and S. Handlin. Penn State University Press, 95–131.

Einstein, K. L., Glick, D. M, and Palmer, M. (2019). *Neighborhood Defenders*. Cambridge University Press.

El-Ghobashy, M. (2021). *Bread and Freedom*. Stanford University Press.

Eulau, H. and Karps, P. D. (1977). "The Puzzle of Representation: Specifying Components of Responsiveness." *Legislative Studies Quarterly* 2(3): 233–254.

Evans, A. (2020). "Overcoming the Global Despondency Trap: Strengthening Corporate Accountability in Supply Chains." *Review of International Political Economy* 27(3): 658–685.

Evans, P. (1997). "The Eclipse of the State? Reflections on Stateness in an Era of Globalization." *World Politics* 50(1): 62–87.

Fowkes, J. (2016). *Building the Constitution*. Cambridge University Press.

Fox, J. (2015). "Social Accountability: What does the Evidence Really Say?" *World Development* 72: 346–361.

Gallagher, J. K. (2017). "The Last Mile Problem: Activists, Advocates, and the Struggle for Justice in Domestic Courts." *Comparative Political Studies* 50(12): 1666–1698.

(2023). *Bootstrap Justice*. Oxford University Press.

Gallagher, M. E. (2006). "Mobilizing the Law in China: 'Informed Disenchantment' and the Development of Legal Consciousness." *Law & Society Review* 40(4): 783–816.

(2017). *Authoritarian Legality in China*. Cambridge University Press.

Galanter, M. (1974). "Why the 'Haves' Come out Ahead: Speculations on the Limits of Legal Change." *Law & Society Review* 9(1): 95–160.

Garay, C., Palmer-Rubin, B., and Poertner, M. (2020). "Organizational and Partisan Brokerage of Social Benefits: Social Policy Linkages in Mexico." *World Development* 136, 105103.

Garay, C. (2016). *Social Policy Expansion in Latin America*. Cambridge University Press.

Gaventa, J. (2021). "Linking the Prepositions: Using Power Analysis to Inform Strategies for Social Action." Journal of Political Power 14(1): 109–130.

González-Ocantos, E. A. (2016). *Shifting Legal Visions*. Cambridge University Press.

Gould, J. B. and Barclay, S. (2012). "Mind the Gap: The Place of Gap Studies in Sociolegal Scholarship." *Annual Review of Law and Social Science* 8(1): 323–335.

Grossman, G., and Slough, T. (2022). "Government Responsiveness in Developing Countries." *Annual Review of Political Science 25*: 131–153.

Gupta, A. (2012). *Red Tape: Bureaucracy, Structural Violence, and Poverty in India*. Duke University Press.

Gulzar, S. and Pasquale, B. (2017). "Politicians, Bureaucrats, and Development: Evidence from India." *American Political Science Review 111*(1): 162–183.

Hacker, J. S. and Pierson, P. (2019). "Policy Feedback in an Age of Polarization." *The Annals of the American Academy of Political and Social Science* 685(1): 8–28.

Harvey, D. (2007). *A Brief History of Neoliberalism*. Oxford University Press.

Heller, P. (2013). *Challenges and Opportunities Civil Society in a Globalizing World*. New York:United Nations Development Programme.

(2019). "Divergent Trajectories of Democratic Deepening: Comparing Brazil, India, and South Africa." *Theory and Society 48*(3): 351–382.

Heller, P. Mukhopadhyay, P., Banda, S., & Sheikj, S. (2015). Exclusion, Informality, and Predation in the Cities of Delhi. Working Paper. New Delhi: Centre for Policy Research.

Heller, P., Swaminathan, S., and Varshney, A. (2023). "The Rich Have Peers, the Poor Have Patrons: Engaging the State in a South Indian City." *American Journal of Sociology* 129(1): 76–122.

Helmke, G. (2005). *Courts under Constraints*. Cambridge University Press.

Hicken, A., and Nathan, N. L. (2020). Clientelism's Red Herrings: Dead Ends and New Directions in the Study of Nonprogrammatic Politics. *Annual Review of Political Science* 23: 277–294.

Holston, J. (2008). *Insurgent Citizenship*. Princeton University Press.

Holland, A. C. (2017). *Forbearance as Redistribution*. Cambridge University Press.

Honig, D. (2021). "Supportive Management Practice and Intrinsic Motivation go together in the Public Service." *Proceedings of the National Academy of Sciences* 118(13): 1–10.

Houtzager, P. P., and Acharya, A. K. (2011). "Associations, Active Citizenship, and the Quality of Democracy in Brazil and Mexico." *Theory and Society 40*: 1–36.

Iversen, T. (2005). *Capitalism, Democracy, and Welfare*. Cambridge University Press.

Jayal, N. (2013). *Citizenship and its Discontents*. Harvard University Press.

Jenkins, R. and Manor, J. (2017). *Politics and the Right to Work*. Oxford University Press.

Kapiszewski, D., Levitsky, S., and Yashar, D. (2021). *The Inclusionary Turn in Latin American Democracies*. Cambridge University Press.

Kitschelt, H., and Wilkinson, S. (2007). *Patrons, Clients and Policies: Patterns of Democratic Accountability and Political Competition*. Cambridge University Press.

Krishna, A. (2011). "Gaining Access to Public Services and the Democratic State in India:Institutions in the Middle." *Studies in Comparative International Development* 46 (1): 98–117.

Krishna, A., Rains, E., and Wibbels, E. (2020). "Negotiating Informality–Ambiguity, Intermediation, and a Patchwork of Outcomes in Slums of Bengaluru." *The Journal of Development Studies* 56(11): 1983–1999.

Kruks-Wisner, G. (2018a). *Claiming the State*. Cambridge University Press.

(2018b). "The Pursuit of Social Welfare: Citizen Claim-making in Rural India." *World Politics* 70(1): 122–163.

(2021). "Great Expectations, Great Grievances: The Politics of Citizens' Complaints in India." *Comparative Politics* 54(1): 27-49.

(2022). "Social Brokerage: Accountability and the Social Life of Information." *Comparative Political Studies* 55(14): 2382–2415.

Kruks-Wisner, G. and Kumar, T. (2023). *Voice and Response: Citizens and Bureaucrats at the Frontlines of Local Democracy*. EGAP Registration.

Kumar, T. (2022). "Home Price Subsidies Increase Local-Level Political Participation in Urban India." *The Journal of Politics*, *84*(2), 831-845.

Lamprea, E. (2015). *Derechos en la práctica*. Universidad de los Andes.

Lamprea, E. and García, J. (2016). "Closing the Gap between Formal and Material Health Care Coverage in Colombia." *Health and Human Rights Journal 18(2): 49–65*.

Landau, D. (2010). "Political Institutions and Judicial Role in Comparative Constitutional Law." *Harvard International Law Journal* 51: 319–378.

(2014). "Beyond Judicial Independence: The Construction of Judicial Power in Colombia." doctoral Dissertation, Harvard University.

Locke, R. M. and Thelen, K. (1995). "Apples and Oranges Revisited: Contextualized Comparisons and the Study of Comparative Labor Politics." *Politics & Society* 23(3): 337–367.

Lozano, R., Fullman, N., Mumford, J. E. et al. (2020). "Measuring Universal Health Coverage Based on an Index of Effective Coverage of Health Services in 204 Countries and Territories, 1990–2019." *The Lancet* 396-(10258): 1250–1284.

Lueders, H. (2021). "Electoral Responsiveness in Closed Autocracies: Evidence from Petitions in the Former German Democratic Republic." *American Political Science Review* 116(3): 827–842.

MacLean, L. M. (2011). "State Retrenchment and the Exercise of Citizenship in Africa." *Comparative Political Studies* 44(9): 1238–1266.

Mangla, A. (2015). "Bureaucratic Norms and State Capacity in India: Implementing Primary Education in the Himalayan Region." *Asian Survey* 55(5): 882–908.

(2022). *Making Bureaucracy Work*. Cambridge University Press.

Mann, M. (1984). "The Autonomous Power of the State: Its Origins, Mechanisms and Results." *European Journal of Sociology* 25(2): 185–213.

Mansuri, G. and Rao, V. (2013). *Localizing Development*. The World Bank.

Marshall, T. H. (1950). *Citizenship and Social Class*. Cambridge University Press.

Massoud, M. F. (2013). *Law's Fragile State*. Cambridge University Press.

Maynard-Moody, S. and Musheno, M. (2000). "State Agent or Citizen Agent: Two Narratives of Discretion." *Journal of Public Administration Research and Theory: J-PART* 10(2): 329–358.

McAdam, D., Tarrow, S., and Tilly, C. (2001). *Dynamics of Contention*. Cambridge University Press.

McCann, M. and Kahraman, F. (2021). "On the Interdependence of Liberal and Illiberal/Authoritarian Legal Forms in Racial Capitalist Regimes." *Annual Review of Law and Social Science* 17(1): 483–503.

Merino, R. (2020). "The Cynical State: Forging Extractivism, Neoliberalism and Development in Governmental Spaces." *Third World Quarterly* 41(1): 58–76.

Mettler, S. and Soss, J. (2004). "The Consequences of Public Policy for Democratic Citizenship: Bridging Policy Studies and Mass Politics." *Perspectives on Politics* 2(1): 55–73.

Mettler, S. and Sorelle, M. (2018). "Policy Feedback Theory." In *Theories of the Policy Process*. Edited by Christopher Weible and Paula Sabatier. Routledge, 103–134.

Michelson, E. (2007). "Climbing the Dispute Pagoda: Grievances and Appeals to the Official Justice System in Rural China." *American Sociological Review* 72(3): 459–485.

Michener, J. (2018). *Fragmented Democracy*. Cambridge University Press.

Mooij, J. and Dev, M. (2004). "Social Sector Priorities: An Analysis of Budgets and Expenditures in India in the 1990s." https://papers.ssrn.com/abstract=513446.

Moyn, S. (2010). *The Last Utopia*. Belknap Press.

Muralidharan, K., Niehaus, P., and Sukhtankar, S. (2023). "General Equilibrium Effects of (improving) Public Employment Programs: Experimental Evidence from India." *Econometrica* 91(4): 1261–1295.

Murillo, V. M. (2000). "From Populism to Neoliberalism: Labor Unions and Market Reforms in Latin America." *World Politics* 52(2): 135–168.

Murtazashvili J. (2016). *Informal Order and the State in Afghanistan*. Cambridge University Press.

Nathan, N. (2023). *The Scarce State*. Cambridge University Press.

National Department of Human Settlements. (2017). "Annual Performance Plan 2017/2018." On file with authors. https://www.dhs.gov.za/sites/default/files/annual_reports/DHS%20APP_2017-2018_ANNEX_G.pdf

Nayar, B. R. (2009). *The Myth of the Shrinking State* . Oxford University Press.

Nichter, S. (2018). *Votes for Survival*. Cambridge University Press.

O'Brien, K. (1996). "Rightful Resistance." *World Politics* 49(1): 31–55.

O'Brien, K, and Li, L. (2006). *Rightful Resistance in Rural China*. Cambridge University Press.

O'Donnell, G. (1993). "On the State, Democratization and Some Conceptual Problems." *World Development* 21(8): 1355–1369.

Peruzzotti, E. and Smulovitz, C. (2006). *Enforcing the Rule of Law*. University of Pittsburgh Press.

Pierson, P. (1993). "When Effect Becomes Cause: Policy Feedback and Political Change." *World Politics* 45(4): 595–628.

Pritchett, L. (2009). Is India a Flailing State?: Detours on the Four Lane Highway to Modernization. Working Paper.

Ray, D. (2003). *Aspirations, Poverty, and Economic Change*. New York University.

Roberts, K. (2021). "The Inclusionary Turn and Its Political Limitations." In *The Inclusionary Turn in Latin American Democracies*. Edited by Kapiszewski, D., Levitsky, S., & Yashar, D. Cambridge University Press, 518–538.

(2022). "Temporal Distance, Reactive Sequences, and Institutional Legacies: Reflections on Latin America's Neoliberal Critical Junctures." Unpublished manuscript.

Robinson, N. (2013). *Complaining to the State: Grievance Redress and India's Social Welfare Programs*. Center for the Advanced Study of India.

Rodríguez Garavito, C. A. (2011). "Beyond the Courtroom: The Impact of Judicial Activism on Socioeconomic Rights in Latin America." *Texas Law Review* 89: 1669–1698.

Scheppele, K. L. (2013). "The Rule of Law and the Frankenstate: Why Governance Checklists Do Not Work." *Governance* 26(4): 559–562.

Seekings, J. (2005). *Prospects for Basic Income in Developing Countries: A Comparative Analysis of Welfare Regimes in the South.* University of Cape Town.

Simmons, E. (2014). "Grievances Do Matter in Mobilization." *Theory and Society* 43(5): 513–546.

(2016). *Meaningful Resistance.* Cambridge University Press.

Simmons, E., and Smith, N. (2017). "Comparison with an Ethnographic Sensibility." *PS: Political Science & Politics* 50(1): 126–130.

Singh, P. (2015). *How Solidarity Works for Welfare.* Cambridge University Press.

Socio-Economic Rights Institute of South Africa (SERI). (2020). "Adequate Temporary Alternative Accommodation." https://www.seri-sa.org/images/Policy_brief_2_AA_Final.pdf

Soifer, H. and vom Hau, M. (2008). "Unpacking the Strength of the State: The Utility of State Infrastructural Power." *Studies in Comparative International Development* 43(3): 219–230.

Soss, J. and Schram, S. F. (2007). "A Public Transformed? Welfare Reform as Policy Feedback." *American Political Science Review* 101(1): 111–127.

Statistics South Africa. (2016). "Community Survey 2016: Statistical Release." http://cs2016.statssa.gov.za/wp-content/uploads/2016/07/NT-30-06-2016-RELEASE-for-CS-2016-_Statistical-releas_1-July-2016.pdf.

(2020). "General Household Survey 2020: Statistical Release." www.statssa.gov.za/publications/P0318/P03182020.pdf.

Stern, R. (2013). *Environmental Litigation in China.* Cambridge University Press.

Stokes, S., Dunning, T., Nazareno, M., and Brusco, V. (2013). *Brokers, Voters, and Clientelism.* Cambridge University Press.

Sukhtankar, S. (2017). "India's National Rural Employment Guarantee Scheme: What Do We Really Know about the World's Largest Workfare Program?" *Brookings-NCAE India Policy Forum* 13(1), 231–285.

Suttner, R. (2012). "The African National Congress Centenary: A Long and Difficult Journey." *International Affairs* 88(4): 719–738.

Tait, K. (2021). Roadblocks to Access: Perceptions of Law and Socioeconomic Problems in South Africa. Doctoral dissertation, University of Massachusetts Amherst.

Tait, K. and Taylor, W. K. (2023). "The Possibility of Rights Claim-Making in Court." *Law & Social Inquiry* 48(3): 1023–1052.

Tarrow, S. (1998). *Power in Movement.* Cambridge university press.

Taylor, W. K. (2018). "Ambivalent Legal Mobilization: Perceptions of Justice and the Use of the Tutela in Colombia." *Law & Society Review* 52(2): 337–367.

(2020a). "On the Social Construction of Legal Grievances: Evidence From Colombia and South Africa." *Comparative Political Studies* 53(8): 1326–1356.

(2020b). "Constitutional Rights and Social Welfare: Exploring Claims-Making Practices in Post-Apartheid South Africa." *Comparative Politics* 53(1): 25–48.

(2023a). *The Social Constitution: Embedding Social Rights Through Legal Mobilization*. Cambridge University Press.

(2023b) "Judicial Agency and the Adjudication of Social Rights." Human Rights Quarterly 45(2): 283–305.

Uprimny Yepes, R. (2006). "The Enforcement of Social Rights by the Colombian Constitutional Court: Cases and Debates." In *Courts and Social Transformation in New Democracies*. Edited by Robrto Gargarella, R., Roux, T., & Domingo, P. Routledge, 127–152.

Uprimny Yepes, R., and Durán, J. (2014). "Equidad y protección judicial del derecho a la salud en Colombia." *197 CEPAL – Serie Políticas Sociales* 1–68.

Veeraraghavan, R. (2022). *Patching Development*. Oxford University Press.

Walter, A. (2018). Petitioning Saddam: Voices from the Iraqi Archives. In A. Russell (ed.), *Truth, Silence and Violence in Emerging States*, 127–146. Routledge.

Weitz-Shapiro, R. (2014). *Curbing Clientelism in Argentina*. Cambridge University Press.

World Bank. (2004). *Making Services Work for the Poor*. World Bank Group.

Acknowledgments

We thank Anindita Adhikari, Adam Auerbach, Alisha Holland, Lisa Hilbink, Rehan Jamil, Diana Kapiszewski, Monika Lemke Pietka, Emily Rains, Blair Read, Ken Roberts, Hillel Soifer, Rachel Stern, Sid Tarrow, and Rebecca Weitz-Shapiro, as well as the participants of the 2022 Princeton Conference on Statebuilding and Political Development, including Anna Gryzmala-Busse, Kimuli Kasara, Melissa Lee, Jen Brick Murtazashvili, David Stasavage, Pavi Suryanarayan, Megan Stewart, and Guillermo Toral, and the series editors, Ben Ross Schneider and Rachel Beatty Riedl, as well as two anonymous reviewers, for their generous feedback and support of this project.

Cambridge Elements ≡

Politics of Development

Rachel Beatty Riedl

Einaudi Center for International Studies and Cornell University

Rachel Beatty Riedl is the Director and John S. Knight Professor of the Einaudi Center for International Studies and Professor in the Government Department and School of Public Policy at Cornell University. Riedl is the author of the award-winning *Authoritarian Origins of Democratic Party Systems in Africa* (2014) and co-author of *From Pews to Politics: Religious Sermons and Political Participation in Africa* (with Gwyneth McClendon, 2019). She studies democracy and institutions, governance, authoritarian regime legacies, and religion and politics in Africa. She serves on the Editorial Committee of World Politics and the Editorial Board of African Affairs, Comparative Political Studies, Journal of Democracy, and Africa Spectrum. She is co-host of the podcast Ufahamu Africa.

Ben Ross Schneider

Massachusetts Institute of Technology

Ben Ross Schneider is Ford International Professor of Political Science at MIT and Director of the MIT-Brazil program. Prior to moving to MIT in 2008, he taught at Princeton University and Northwestern University. His books include *Business Politics and the State in 20th Century Latin America* (2004), *Hierarchical Capitalism in Latin America* (2013), *Designing Industrial Policy in Latin America: Business-Government Relations and the New Developmentalism* (2015), and *New Order and Progress: Democracy and Development in Brazil* (2016). He has also written on topics such as economic reform, democratization, education, labor markets, inequality, and business groups.

Advisory Board

Yuen Yuen Ang, *University of Michigan*
Catherine Boone, *London School of Economics*
Melani Cammett, *Harvard University* (former editor)
Stephan Haggard, *University of California, San Diego*
Prerna Singh, *Brown University*
Dan Slater, *University of Michigan*

About the Series

The Element series *Politics of Development* provides important contributions on both established and new topics on the politics and political economy of developing countries. A particular priority is to give increased visibility to a dynamic and growing body of social science research that examines the political and social determinants of economic development, as well as the effects of different development models on political and social outcomes.

Cambridge Elements $\equiv$

Politics of Development

Printed in the United States
by Baker & Taylor Publisher Services